Defending Hope

Defending Hope

Natalie Proudfoot

Printed in the United States of America
ISBN-13: 978-0615625034 (proudliving press)
ISBN-10: 0615625037

GRATEFUL ACKNOWLEDGEMENT IS MADE FOR THE USE OF THE FOLLOWING:

Quote by Maya Angelou.

Quote by Aristotle.

"Hope Is the Thing with Feathers" by Emily Dickenson.

"Measure for Measure" by William Shakespeare.

"Walden" by Henry David Thoreau.

Quote by Mark Twain.

Dedicated to the millions of brave men, women, and children, their families and extended support systems who have weathered the news.

Half the proceeds of *Defending Hope* will benefit the American Cancer Society.

Author's Note

When I started writing Hope's story a few years ago, I had no idea it would become my own.

On Friday, March 9, 2012, I was diagnosed with cancer in my right breast: Ductal carcinoma in suta (DCIS), a very early, very treatable form of breast cancer, which, in my case, would require a mastectomy, the surgical removal of my breast.

My first instinct was to call a doctor in Indianapolis for a second opinion (denial), then to rage about my impending loss (anger), then to plead with God to spare my breast: "I'll be good, I promise!" (bargaining), followed by a withdrawal into myself (depression), and, finally, an acceptance of my disease, prognosis, and treatment.

Actually, I didn't move through the stages of grief in a linear fashion – I dipped my toe into each for brief periods of time, haphazardly, much like Hope. In fact, I found myself relating with Hope's journey, feeling comforted knowing that I was not alone in my mix of emotions.

I also decided to pay attention to Dr. Ellie's wise counsel: in order to experience hope I would need to create hope. So, I decided to self-publish *Defending Hope* on April 30, 2012, the same date as my surgery.

It turns out I wrote my own story: not exactly, but close enough. Perhaps, I wrote yours too: not exactly, of course, but close enough. Hope and grief are intermingled in frightening and beautiful ways, unique to each one of us.

I hope that this book provides you the same comfort, encouragement, and sense of normalcy it did for me in a time of need.

With love and lots of hope,
Natalie

Hope is that thing with feathers
That perches in the soul.
And sings the tune
Without the words,
and never stops at all.
-Emily Dickinson

PART I - *Fall*

Chapter 1

Last night I dreamed I was floating down the Nile River on a big banana tree leaf, the leafy fronds curled up around me in a big embrace. On the banks of the swiftly moving river, the native people were clapping, laughing, and smiling with big toothless grins. Men and women alike wore neck rings and ear plugs, all were swathed in brightly colored wraps. The colors blinded me and the hot sun beat down on my body in an intensity I had never known. I tried to paddle over to the bank but gravity kept pulling me north, toward the unknown.

As I woke up, still a little groggy from the vivid experience of my dream, I thought of how my dad would read to me from his coveted, gold-framed *National Geographic* magazines, specifically remembering a story about the Nile. At the time I thought that something divine must have caused a river to flow north. I was just a kid then and now I know the truth: simple gravity. That the mountains in the middle of the African continent force the river downhill.

I also recalled how Dad read to me about a tribe of indigenous people in the Nile Valley who wait until their children turn five before naming them. If I remember correctly, the purpose of waiting is to get a sense of what each child has to offer the world before assigning a name. At the time I found it funny, that it would be really hard to go through the first five years of life as 'Hey you' or whatever their native tongue translation of 'Yo, no-name' might be. Now that I'm changing my name, though, the whole concept makes a lot of sense.

It's not easy to be saddled with a name like Hope when you are learning the hard way about pain and suffering. We moved from California to Ohio four months ago when we found out that Dad's lung cancer was Stage III. I also learned that as the stages go up, the chances of my dad surviving go down.

I'm Hope because my parents believed in it. Still do, in spite of everything. Somehow my older brother snuck by with Milo, a name meaning mild, or easy-going. Anyone would agree it fits him perfectly. But Hope?

Those happy, toothless people on the riverbank must have been standing together in a greeting, preparing for a coming-of-age ceremony in which the world welcomes the new me, leaving the old behind.

ॐ

My mom grew up in Youngstown, Ohio, which is why we're here now. In fact, Grandma still lives in the same house Mom grew up in, though Aunt Susan, Uncle Dave, and my cousins Lily and Henry moved into a "fancy" new neighborhood on the north side of town a couple of years ago after living in Arizona. (Fancy is Mom's word, not mine.)

Lily is five months older than me, but a whole grade ahead because of the way our birthdays fall. Mine is in August and Lily's is in March. She is one of those really perky, cheerleader-types, which is usually fine, but when fun is the last thing on your mind, she can be just plain annoying. She truly wants to be helpful by introducing me to all her friends at school, but I'm really not up for meeting anyone new right now. Don't get me wrong, I'm not opposed to fun. I used to be fun - loads of fun.

Not Henry, though. He's three, therefore a real pain. He cries a lot and throws temper tantrums when he doesn't get his way. I don't know how Lily can stand it, but she's always telling me how cute and sweet he is. As if a three year-old could ever be anyone's idea of a good time. Anyway, Aunt Susan and Uncle Dave sometimes ask if I want to come over and watch Henry when they want to catch a movie or grab a bite to eat. I said yes once and while I was there Henry took the Reese's Cup I had been saving for dessert out of my jeans jacket pocket and ate it. He also tore some pages out of Lily's science book. I'm pretty sure I won't be watching him again anytime soon. At least not until he acts a little more human and less primate.

Grandma spends lots of time at our house cooking meals, which is great because she makes the best chicken cacciatore I've ever tasted. She also makes incredible desserts: brownies, cakes, homemade pudding. You name it. Sometimes I think she's just trying to sugar-coat everything for us, and I have to say that it works pretty well. One bite of Grandma's gooey caramel brownies and sometimes even I forget about the reason we now live in the Midwest.

Even though my mom has lived on the West Coast since college, we've returned to her family. I think she is counting on them to get us through this ordeal. Probably so she can escape us, just like she has always done.

5

My dad grew up in Pennsylvania, which is a whole state away, but only twenty minutes from my house. It's kind of strange to think that it takes four hours to drive to Cedar Point, but I can be in the land of "Virtue, Liberty, and Independence" in mere minutes. Not that I have much need to travel there, since Dad's parents both died before I was even born. He has an aunt I have met once and a couple of cousins I've never seen, but no brothers or sisters. I guess my grandparents thought Dad was simply perfect. Either that or he acted too much like Henry and they decided one kid was more than enough.

From what Dad says, his parents were the strict-type. Parents can be classified three ways: strict, pushover, and absentee. If you are lucky, you have one strict parent and one pushover. This combination means that you have one parent looking out for your best interest, which is code for, "I don't want you wandering off and getting yourself kidnapped." Or, "You can't have a trampoline because you'll fall and break your leg."

Because you understand pretty early on that your strict parent will say no to anything remotely exciting, you quickly learn to ask your pushover parent to do things like ride your bike to the store by yourself or ask for a skateboard for your birthday.

I have witnessed first-hand all the other combinations. On of my friends, D'Shea, back in California, had two strict parents who were always scared out of their minds about something happening to her. She was their only child, which probably didn't help the matter, but D'Shea was never allowed to go to other kids' houses, which sounds really awful, but her parents made sure she had everything a kid might want: cell phone, iPad, swimming pool. I know it sounds really great but, trust me, she was not the happiest person I've ever met.

Lanie, one of the girls I met at school a few weeks ago, seems to have two pushover parents. The reason I think so is that when Lanie wanted to go meet Josh, a tenth-grader, at the movies, they not only said yes, but dropped her off at the theater! Personally, I don't think a thirteen year-old has any business hanging out with sixteen year-old boys, especially after what Lanie told me she and Josh did during the movie. Let's just say they spent more time watching each other's lips than the movie.

The worst kind of parent is the absentee-type. The reason I know is because before Dad's diagnosis my mom fit this description perfectly. She was always gone, either at work or in the woods. My mom is a biologist who lived and worked among the giant sequoia trees, you know, the ones they always show in National Geographic specials where the person standing in front of them takes on the appearance of a dwarf (or "little person", as Mom would insist).

She loves those redwood trees, and spent most of her time trying to understand their delicate ecosystem and protecting them from forces outside of their control (namely humans). I've never met anyone so passionate about her work. Actually, for Mom it wasn't even work, it was her purpose.

"Sequoias provide us with life," she said to me one time. "The oxygen given off by these gracious giants not only provides the very stuff of life to those leeches in Southern California, but they suffer silently with the mass quantity of carbon dioxide they receive in return."

One thing you could say about Mom, she never minces words.

Moving to Ohio served a practical purpose too, because Mom got a job teaching biology at Youngstown State University. She tried her hand at teaching once before, out in California, before I was born, but was disheartened by the disinterest of her students to the world around them.

"I didn't mind the questioners or even the doubters," she told me once of her non-environmentally-minded students, required to take Biology 101 to fulfill the general requirements. "They cared enough to voice their opinion, and I appreciated that. What I couldn't take was the empty seats. The students who didn't show up half the time yet eeked by with a C minus. I just couldn't stand that kind of apathy."

I think she and Dad knew that the only way to get her out of the forest and back into our lives was to move across the country where Oaks, Maples, and Hickories are bountiful and thriving, and sequoias are a giant, distant memory. As far as apathy goes, I think Mom is secretly hoping for empty seats.

Mom "compromised her principles" and bought a beautiful bowl made from the trunk of a "lost redwood" before we moved. I asked her how a tree can become lost and she rolled her eyes.

"It pains me to know that someone is profiting from my purchase," she said, "but I need it as a reminder of all that good, hard work."

She may have been talking about the bowl, but I'm not sure. Either way, she never answered my question.

Honestly, I never really minded not having Mom around that much until we moved to Ohio when, all of a sudden, I was bumping into her in the kitchen each morning. She's a fine person and all, but I secretly hate her right now.

I hate her because she's the one I'm used to living without.

Chapter 2

Our rental house is pretty close to campus, but far enough away that our neighbors are closer to my parents' age than Milo's or mine. The house is actually bigger than the house back in California. In California everything is overpriced, especially land, with so many people competing for it. Here in Ohio, the lots are much bigger – we have actual grass to mow, for example. We have trees and flowers, or at least the remains of flowers. It being September, I'm not really sure what popped up last spring, but there are a few brown stems here and there, which tells me that, come March, we'll have at least a few blooms.

The house itself is nothing extraordinary: living room, kitchen, three bedrooms, two bathrooms. I do have my own bedroom, though, which was non-negotiable. I don't think my parents would have required me to room with my brother, being that we're both teenagers, but you never know. Sometimes desperate times call for desperate measures.

I love the living room. It has these dark brown hardwood floors with a light brown intricate border around the outside of the room. It's worn, but the scratches only make me curious about all of the other renters who lived here. Or maybe we're the first. Maybe the original owner, a little old lady, had to go live in a nursing home after her kids decided she was too old for the upkeep, as evidenced by the scratches on the floor.

The kitchen is really small, but cozy. It's set up in a u-shape, with the sink at the bottom of the 'u'. The stove is on one arm of the 'u', the refrigerator on the other. Unfortuantely there's no dishwasher, unless you count the two my dad rattled off when we mentioned its absence: Milo and Hope.

Our house back in California was much more compact, but had all the amenities: dishwasher, hot tub, walk-in closets. In fact, my closet was so large that I ended up moving my desk in there when I was trying to concentrate on writing a paper about climate change. Milo's and my bedroom walls butted up to each other, and my desk was along the wall that bordered Milo's Wii. The racket he made playing his video games prompted the moving of the desk, but once I was all settled into my cave, I was quite comfortable there. My desk remained and my grades came up. I don't know if it was just a coincidence, but I can tell you that, since we moved to Ohio, Milo's gaming system was intentionally brought out to the living room, "So that we can spend more time together as a family," my dad said.

In fact, we do seem to be spending much more time together, but I don't know if I would trade it for the life I had before. Living like a cave-dweller worked just fine for me; my retreat to the dark recesses had nothing to do with fear or illness.

That was a voluntary holing-up. This is a black hole.

I used to love lots of things, including school. As you can tell, I'm smart, for one. I also like to be right. Teachers either love that about me or hate it. I attribute it to confidence. Teachers are people, after all, and some are better at accepting the fact that they don't know everything. They simply can't.

I don't know everything either, but at least I can admit it.

I had a teacher in fourth grade, back in California, who hated me. Well, my dad said that she didn't hate me, but hated my willingness to call her out. I couldn't help it, her grammar was bad. (That's actually an example of something she might have said.) She also used to threaten the class with, "If anyone says one more word during the math lesson without holding up their hand, each one of you will stay in during recess and write sentences."

Mariah coughed.

"That's it!" she shouted, "Recess is out, sentences are in!"

"Um, Mrs. Marten, that was actually a cough, not a word," I said, defender of all that was unjust.

"You're right, Hope, you're right," she said, slowly shaking her head. "Thank you for pointing that out. You have convinced me to rethink it. Class, you are all welcome to enjoy your recess. All of you except Hope, that is."

It was like that all year, but as much as I complained to my dad, he just smiled and told me it was a good learning experience for me. That someday I would understand.

All I understood at the time was that my teacher hated me and my dad didn't care enough to step in and change her mind.

This year, though, I figured out really quickly who the insecure teachers were. (You can tell by how often they threaten the class and then don't follow through.) I made it my mission to be on my best behavior during these classes, to really kiss up. I offered to help pass out papers. I helped the students who were too stupid to take adequate notes. I would have offered to bang erasers together, if we still used them. Instead I offered to go to the office to request new dry-erase markers when the current markers wore out, their ink written and erased many times over on the large white boards in the front of the classrooms.

It's funny, really, that these teachers think so highly of me. What they don't know is that I'm doing it out of pity for them. I don't think they are at all prepared for the amount of trouble I could give them if I really wanted to. They have no idea who I really am. Who Hope really is.

Because I'm trouble, I really am. With a capital "T."

Chapter 3

I knew my parents wouldn't take me seriously if I happened to casually mention that I was a bit tired of my name and wanted something more exciting. The truth was that ever since Dad's diagnosis, I felt like everyone was looking at me differently. Expectantly. Like I was the lucky rabbit's foot tucked away in their back pocket.

Hope is a great philosophy, in theory, and I'm usually all for it. But when it feels like your entire family is looking to you to lead them through the unknown, it's like a huge boulder lying upon your chest, pushing the breath of life right out of your lungs and into the universe for everyone to snatch up.

Changing my name would take some guts and gusto. And my own initiative.

So I called the county courthouse. Since the phone book didn't list a "Change Your Name" department, I dialed the judge directly.

"Judge Mann's office. Barb speaking. How can I help you?"

"Um, hi. My name is Hope Wallace and I'm trying to find out how to change my name."

"Are you recently married?" Barb asked.

"Ha! I mean no. No, I'm not married, I want to change my first name," I answered with a grin, excited that Barb thought I sounded really old.

"How old are you?" she asked, now suspicious.

"I'm thirteen, but most people say I'm really mature for my age," I said. "Look, I know you probably think I'm just some dumb kid who doesn't know any better, but I *am* going to change my name. Can you just tell me what I need to do?"

I would need to pay court fees, which would cost just over three-hundred dollars, and I would need a legal guardian's signed consent to move forward. She said she would speak with Judge Mann and get back with me. Her final remark to me not only proved my point, but gave me a little ammunition, which I was certain I would need in the coming weeks.

"You know what I think? I think you are already one lucky girl. I wish I had a name like Hope. A name with meaning. Barb is a fine name, but it sure never inspired anyone."

ℰℭ

My parents have hired a therapist for me.

"Do you think I'm crazy?" I accused.

"Hopie, nobody thinks you're crazy," Dad said, "but we are concerned about you. The move has been tough and you don't seem very interested in trying to make it work."

"You mean like Mom has been," I threw right back, knowing it

14

would sting. Mom has been like a zombie moving through the house. Usually people get lost in the woods, but not Mom. The woods are her retreat. She's seems lost within the confines of these walls.

"Honey, we got a good recommendation from Aunt Susan," said Mom, ignoring my sarcasm. "I just really think you need someone right now."

She was right about that.

What I didn't understand, though, was why me? Why not Mom? Dad? Milo? He was the one they should be worried about, going about his normal routine, playing soccer, making friends left and right as if nothing unusual was happening. Milo was clearly in denial.

I was just being reasonable. If there was a way to escape the burden, the pressure of Hope, then I was sure going to check it out. I didn't really get why it impacted my parents anyway.

I understood that they had picked out my name. That, when I arrived all pink and slimy and full of promise, my parents took one look at me and thought, "Hope. We'll call her Hope."

I mean, yes, after thirteen years it would be an adjustment. People were bound to forget and call me "Hope," occasionally, but in time we would all adjust. It was *my* name, after all. Why couldn't it be *my* decision?

Chapter 4

It's Wednesday, which means I'm going to see Dr. Ellie after school.

I talked to her on the phone when Mom called to schedule the appointment.

"Yes, every other Wednesday works for Hope. Three thirty? Yes, I think we can make that work. Hope? Um, yes, she's here. Sure, just a moment."

"Hope," Mom whispered, pushing the phone up against her chest to cover the receiver. "Dr. Ellie would like to speak with you for a minute."

She goes by Dr. Ellie, the way you might call your preschool teacher "Miss Jenny". Her real name is Eleanor R. Boskovicz, Ph.D., but I suppose she thinks it might be hard to tell a Dr. Boskovicz all of your deepest, darkest secrets, and she's probably right, although most of my friends and family would agree that I've never had a problem

17

saying what's on my mind. It's what my dad calls "my secret weapon."

From what I understand, a secret weapon is a positive trait or feature that is helpful, so I have no clue why he says this, seeing as how I'm constantly sticking my foot in my mouth and saying stupid things to people I care about. He calls this "growing pains" and says someday my heart and head will work together as one unit.

It's a rush to get to my appointment with Dr. Ellie. I jump off the bus and wave goodbye to Doug, my bus driver, who never fails to salute back, run inside and make myself a peanut butter and brown sugar sandwich, and race out the door with Dad so we can drive across town to Dr. Ellie's.

"Ah, Hope," says Dr. Ellie. "It's wonderful to meet you in person."

I like the way she says "ah," sort of dreamily. She dresses a little bit like my mom's friend Luann back in California. Luann is a painter who, when she wasn't wearing her husband's old t-shirts, splattered with remnants of colors with names like ochre, bittersweet, and moss, would wear what I used to call "silks" when I was little. Luann had beautiful clothes that ebbed and flowed with her every movement. She didn't waste her time with neutrals either – everything was vivid.

Dr. Ellie is a little more conservative with her wardrobe, but she is wearing a bright orange tunic with black leggings that add to her likeability. I already feel I can trust this woman who dresses with the same comfortable ease as her big, beautiful smile. Before I know it, I am chatting away as if she is an old friend.

"I'm changing my name," I tell her, right off the bat.

I sit up a little straighter, partly as an encouragement to proceed with my reasoning, and partly because the couch was hitting me funny in my lower back.

"I haven't decided on my new name yet, but it's going to reflect who I am better than Hope," I offer, watching my therapist's face for the same look of disappointment I was so used to seeing on my parent's faces since I brought up the subject with them last month.

Dr. Ellie seemed not to be phased by this revelation.

"I see," she said. "I am sure the library has a variety of baby name books available for loan if you are having difficulty."

I stared at her blankly for a moment, confused at her agreeing with me, and with a moment's regret that my parents were spending good money on these sessions, which, I'm sure, they hoped would result in me dropping the name change plan.

"Uh, yeah, that's a good idea," I said. "I've been making a list of names that I like, but none stand out above the others yet."

"Ah, Hope," said Dr. Ellie, "I think you will find that one day you will simply know, and that will be that. Of course, there is a practical matter involved in changing one's name that you may not have considered. I am not up on Ohio law regarding name change, but, being a minor, I am certain you will need a parent's written consent in order to fulfill your desire."

"That's what Mom said," I quickly shot back.

Just because Dr. Ellie held a Ph.D. didn't mean I wasn't on top of my game, especially one that affected the entire rest of my life.

"I looked it up online and couldn't find the information I needed, so I called down to the county building and left a message for Judge Mann. I talked to his secretary, Barb, and she is going to have him call me. I haven't heard from him yet, but I'm sure he's a busy guy. I'll try back today," I finished, adjusting myself again on the couch, deciding next time to try the rocking chair. It looked a little more comfortable.

"Well, Hope, you are clearly a self-reliant and responsible young woman," Dr. Ellie said, while plucking what appeared to be a cluster of white cat hair from her bright fuchsia blouse.

"I respect your decision to move forward with the process of changing your name, if that is what you believe to be best." Not missing a beat, she added, "Is that what you believe to be best?" while uncrossing her legs and stretching them out in front of her, crossing her ankles instead.

"Yep," I said, "it's what's best."

What I did not say at that moment, and what had been running through the far reaches of my mind, not quite unconsciously, but not entirely in a place I could admit or verbalize in any meaningful way was this: changing my name just might change everything.

"Well then, Hope," said Dr. Ellie with an irritatingly knowing smile, "what would you like to get out of therapy?"

"Uh, I don't really know," I said, as I considered the question. "You seem really nice, and I like your shirt. Mostly my parents told me I would come talk to you to help me cope with all of the changes. You know, dealing with Ohio winters, new school. Stuff like that."

Dr. Ellie smiled slightly, amused, it seemed, at my joke. She waited to speak, almost as if she thought I had more to add. Realizing this was not the case, she finally asked, "And the changes in your father's health?"

"Yeah, that too," I said, looking down at the hangnail on my left index finger. It had snagged this morning as I zipped up my jeans, and only now was it called to my attention as a flaw that needed to be remedied. I pulled at the hangnail until it tore away from the solid base of the nail. It began bleeding a split-second later and I popped the finger into my mouth, tasting the metallic bite of my own blood. Realizing I was being observed by the good doctor, I quickly removed my finger and discreetly squeezed at the wound in an attempt to stop the bleeding.

"One thing I think is important for my clients to do during

20

therapy is to keep a journal. Have you ever done that?" she asked, forgoing mentioning the self-mutilation she had just witnessed.

"Sure, I have a diary," I said. "I used to write in it every day, but I've kind of gotten out of the habit."

"I would like for you, if you are able, to start fresh with a new journal. It will be a bit different than your daily diary. I think you will find it helpful to jot down your feelings surrounding all of the changes we discussed. In fact, I would suggest making a column for each of the big events that are going on for you right now: 'School,' 'Friends,' 'Dad,' 'Hope.' I encourage you to write down not only the way you feel about each of these topics on a daily basis, but also your response to these feelings."

She must have noticed my confusion because she clarified with, "Your behavior, Hope. What you do when you feel a certain way. We all have coping mechanisms to deal with difficult situations. I think it would be useful for you to see how you cope."

I left the office a few minutes later absolutely drained. Part of me felt invaded. I got the feeling that Dr. Ellie was on to me. Sure, she was nice and seemed to support my name change. On the other hand, I was certain that she, like every other adult I had ever met, believed that I was just a kid who couldn't make a good decision to save her life. I shuffled out of Dr. Ellie's office not only tired, but with a throbbing finger and a bad taste in my mouth.

Chapter 5

I used to think only smokers got cancer because that's what my teachers always said: "Don't smoke or you'll end up with cancer." Well, Dad never smoked. Actually, it was Mom who admitted to me that she took a few puffs back in high school, so what do they know?

Cancer Can Be Unpredictable, according to the pamphlet I found in Dad's grey windbreaker. Dad's getting lung cancer reminds me of those roulette wheels you find in casinos. I know because we had one at my school carnival back in third grade. It's where you put a marble on a spinning wheel and call out a number. When the wheel stops and the marble lands on the number you called out, you win, which is really against the odds, considering there are like a hundred numbers crowded around the wheel.

So at school when my purple marble landed on twenty-two, my lucky number, I won a bike, a shiny, red Schwinn donated by Mr.

Borden, my friend Beth's dad, who owned a bike shop downtown.

Sometimes it seems like my dad's marble landed on his lucky number, but instead of a bike, he won cancer.

Dad had his first round of chemo back in California. Dr. Roland confirmed that there were two malignant tumors on the left lobe of his lung and three on his right. Chemo was tough on Dad. He threw up for days, had no appetite for weeks, and, worst of all, he lost his hair. He tried to be cute and funny, making jokes about how he had been thinning on top for years and was about a week away from shaving it all off anyway.

Mom didn't think it was funny. I know this because since my dad's diagnosis, Mom has a new facial expression which she only uses in those times when Dad tries to be funny and tell cancer jokes. Mom's mouth kind of curls up on one side, which sounds more like a smirk, but the look in her eyes gives away the fact that she's trying really hard not to cry.

She didn't give me "the look" when I shaved my eyebrows, though; she laughed and laughed until she really did start crying.

It all started when Dad began losing his hair a few days after his third chemo treatment. My brother suggested that we all shave our heads in solidarity with Dad. I knew I would never do that, though. What a cliché. Besides, I have the most beautiful hair in my family. It's really long with just the right amount of curl. Not so much that it frizzes, but giving me plenty of wave and volume, making it perfect for wearing up or down. My friends back in California were all pretty envious.

So, when Dad lost his hair I made the decision to shave my eyebrows. I thought it would symbolize my support of Dad while maintaining my dignity.

I had no idea how much dignity eyebrows give a face.

After my mom laughed and cried for what seemed like an eternity, she pulled up a website describing the effects of chemo and I learned right there in black and white about how body hair doesn't necessarily fall out during chemotherapy.

Dad did manage to keep his eyebrows and it took about two months for mine to grow back in. I looked like an alien for the first few weeks. It seemed to fit, though, seeing as how it felt like my family had been invaded.

No, it wasn't by UFO's and little green space creatures, but more an invasion of privacy. Our contained little lives turned upside down to make way for this new, aggressive, mean-spirited force creeping around inside my dad's body.

Cancer had touched down on our little world.

Ω

My dad is literally an everyday hero. He's a public defender. Or at least he was, back in California. He doesn't work now, at least not yet. I have faith that he'll be back at it, though, once his cancer is in remission.

If your image of public defenders is what you see on TV, you're way off base. I asked him once how he could sleep at night knowing he was helping the guilty get off scot-free.

He laughed. "Guilty?" he asked. "Most of these folks are simply guilty of being a product of their environment. Should a fourteen year-old be walking the streets at night with their homies, knives concealed under the folds of their socks? You and I know how stupid that sounds, but for these kids? It's their way of life. The only way to feel safe in a neighborhood where stray bullets take down babies and grandmothers."

He went on: "I may be able to get these kids a lesser sentence and, in doing so, we see young men emerge with renewed interest in creating a life of purpose. These kids deserve better than what they've been handed, that's for sure."

At the time I had been whining about being the only one in my seventh grade class without a cell phone. I promptly dropped my complaining after he told me about a sixteen year-old boy he was defending who had been accused of murder and tried as an adult due to the charge.

"He didn't do it," said Dad, "but he'll serve the time. I can't defend him because he won't sell out. His buddies were there, no doubt, and one of them deserves to be in prison, but my client is guilty of being loyal, and naive. He'll spend ten years behind bars for a crime he didn't commit."

I couldn't imagine feeling so strongly about someone that I would take the fall for their illegal actions. Especially if it meant spending ten years in prison.

"Can't you do anything?" I asked. "You know the truth."

"Lawyer-client privilege," he said. "Besides, I only suspect Simon is covering. But I suspect very strongly. My parental instics are kicking in, like the time you and Milo dropped the ladder on the van then claimed that a stray cat had run into the garage and knocked it over."

I blushed at the memory, especially at being caught in the lie. "You knew?" I asked.

"Of course I knew," he said, pointing to his temple with his index finger. "Parental instics. Plus, there were purple fingerprints all over the van where you and Milo attempted to buff out the scratches."

"We were fingerpainting. I tried to use the ladder to reach the real paintbrushes," I said. "I was trying to surprise you with a mural, but we abandoned the project after the ladder fell. Sorry I never told you," I said, looking away in shame as the memory of that terrible crunch filled my mind.

"It's okay," Dad said, grabbing me for a hug. "Don't worry, I've been keeping a tally up here," he said, again pointing to his head, "of how much you owe me for that repair."

"You have not," I laughed at him. "That dent is still there!"

"Exactly," he said. "I've been saving up."

"Hey, Hopie," he said, changing the subject, "I heard a good one the other day. Want to hear it?"

My dad loves his lawyer jokes and usually I do too, but he told me one a few months ago that keeps creeping back up into my consciousness:

A lawyer died and found himself at the pearly gates. He was admitted to heaven. He saw saints, martyrs, philanthropists, and all-around great people with harps and wings all being treated very well. To his surprise, he was given a golden harp, special treatment, and a throne near God. He was treated much better than anyone else. He asked, 'Are all lawyers treated like this?' He was answered, 'We don't know. You're the first lawyer who's ever been here!'

"Sure, Dad, let's hear it," I said.

"What's the difference between a catfish and a lawyer?" he asked. I couldn't even imagine.

"One is a scum-sucking bottom-dweller, and the other is a fish."

"Good one, huh," he said, chuckling at his own joke.

"Sure, Dad," I said, "it's a real gut-buster."

Chapter 6

I think adults try and protect kids from sadness, but we already know a lot about it. I am still sad that we had to leave my dog, Bones, back in California, for example, but my parents won't even acknowledge it. I know they miss her too, I heard them say so when they thought I wasn't listening.

I eavesdrop on my parents sometimes. It's easy to listen to them talking, since I can hear them through the vent in my bedroom floor. If I really care about the conversation I turn off the thermostat so the noisy air doesn't blow through the vent at a critical moment. They don't know that I do this, and would probably be really embarrassed to know that I hear other noises coming from their bedroom, but I just put my pillow over my head when they start laughing and cooing, since I know what's coming next.

This morning I tuned in with my ear up against the vent just in time to hear my mom crying.

29

"Nothing about this is fair! Nothing! Dragging the kids across the country least of all!" I heard Mom yelling in a muffled voice.

I couldn't make out what Dad was saying, but he didn't get much of a chance to say anything when Mom interrupted.

"And Hope. Oh God, Hope is just a baby. She's going to be lost without you – don't you understand that!?"

I heard her yelling at my dad about all that he was going to miss: my brother's and my high school graduation, walking me down the aisle at my wedding. I mean, really. The last thing I care about right now is getting married. I don't really even like boys too much yet, except for Johnny Depp, and he's married or at least has a live-in girlfriend and a couple of kids or something.

My mom just doesn't get it and she can't even begin to comprehend what she doesn't get about it. She's the grown-up and she's crying and screaming like a baby. She's yelling at my dad, acting like he asked to be sick. Like he wants to spend his days in pajamas, sleeping and puking.

I pulled out the journal that Dr. Ellie had prompted me to begin. It was blank. No feelings. No behaviors. No words. In fact, now that I opened it up for the first time, I realized that I had even purchased a journal with no lines. *Figures,* I thought, determined to spend some time making the journal more usable.

I began to stand up from the cross-legged position I was sitting in, next to the vent. I hadn't noticed the numbness in my right leg and nearly fell down when it provided little support upon standing. The pins-and-needles sensation quickly followed and I found myself stomping my foot on the ground, trying to get the blood flowing in order to ease the discomfort.

I hobbled over to my desk and opened the middle drawer, sifting through empty gum wrappers, random paper clips, and a fourth grade picture of my brother before he had contacts and still wore little round, gold-framed glasses, until I found my ruler, lying half-under a hodge-podge of awards I had received from school back in California: Student of the Month, Honor Roll, Best Friend Forever. Okay, that last one was handmade by my BFF Abby last year when I was disappointed that poem entitled, "Hope for the Best" was not accepted for publication in an American Girl magazine contest.

Ha! I thought. *How ironic.*

Thinking about Abby made me want to call her, but with a three-hour time difference it was only eight in the morning. I'm pretty sure Abby would not appreciate me waking her up to remind her of my failure to become published.

Instead I grabbed the ruler and sat down at the desk, pushing aside the clutter to make way for my project. I did a visual estimate and determined it was probably fifty pages. I measured the page and did a quick calculation to determine I could fit thirteen lines, spaced half an inch apart, giving me plenty of room to track the multitude of feelings I was experiencing at any given moment. I dozed off, pleased with the progress of my newly lined paper when…

"Hope, Lunch!" Mom yelled up the stairs, waking me abruptly from my cramped position at the desk.

A page of my journal rose up with my cheek, unsticking itself as I sat upright and reoriented myself to my room, having awakened from a familiar dream in which the setting was always wooded. I stood and stretched my arms up, arching my back and glanced down at the newly-lined journal. I opened to page one, the word 'sleepy' headlining the column I had labeled 'Feelings'. Remembering what Dr. Ellie had said about recording my responses, I quickly labeled a second column 'Behaviors' and jotted down 'took a nap'.

Closing the journal, I headed out of the room and down the stairs to enjoy what smelled like chili with a smug feeling of satisfaction for having responded so appropriately to the way I was feeling.

Chapter 7

Thursday, October 21

Hopie,

I love the fall, don't you? The color of the leaves brings back memories of my parents taking me to the pumpkin patch. We didn't have a lot of money, so we had to agree on one pumpkin. Of course I always wanted the biggest, roundest, orangest pumpkin in the patch! I don't remember ever finding it, though. Mom and Dad always convinced me to pick one with some flaw: a dent, discoloration, or missing stem. I remember hating them for it, but now that I look back, I think they were simply preparing me for life. Perfection is false. Embrace your pumpkin, Hope, no matter what!

I love you, Dad

Dad and I have this really cool tradition of writing each other notes and sticking them under the other's pillow. It all started with the tooth fairy. She would leave me little love notes upon collecting one of the twenty teeth I donated to her cause over the years. I lost my last molar in sixth grade and a week later found a note under the pillow signed "Dad." I asked him about it at breakfast and he just grinned and said he couldn't bear someone not telling me how great I am simply because I had all my adult teeth.

We don't write each other notes every day. Maybe once a week I'll find something under the pillow. I've been saving them in an old school notebook, its pages heavily marked with my own chicken-scratch, trying to understand fractions. The note that gives me chills every time I read it is dated March sixth, the day after Dad's diagnosis. It simply says, "I'm scared." I know some parents wouldn't want to worry their kids and admit to being scared, but Dad isn't like that. He treats me like a person, not a little kid.

My notes to Dad aren't very profound, but I want to remind him how much I love him and how brave I think he is. My BFF Abby once told me that she made a pact with God after her grandma had a stroke: if she scored a goal during her soccer game, then her grandma would be all right. She did, which was a huge deal since Abby was terrible at the sport! Anyway, that night her grandma woke up and started talking like nothing had happened.

I figure if there is even a remote possibility that my notes might have an impact bordering on miraculous, I'll keep writing them. If the cancer had even the slightest idea how much I need my dad, it would take a hike.

I grab the note from Dad and stick it in my notebook, right up front. I'm running late for school, as usual, and don't have time to hunt down its rightful spot next to last week's note, in which Dad listed his favorite books of all time: *Walden, The Sneetches, To Kill a Mockingbird, A Tale of Two Cities.*

It must be hard for him now, not reading, not defending his clients. Even though he is physically capable of picking up a book, he isn't, not right now. And because I notice such things, I pointed it out.

"What's wrong, Dad, did you run out of new material?" I joke, sweeping my arm over the massive oak bookshelves that line our living room.

"Hmmm? Oh, no. I just can't seem to get my mind to focus on anything," Dad said.

"Not even Keats?" I asked. Surely he could focus on Keats.

"It's fine, Hopie, it's just not happening right now," he said. "No worries, though, I've discovered daytime TV," he joked. "Ever watch Dr. Phil? What a character."

I ignored the TV reference. Couldn't even go there. "Do you want me to read to you?" I asked

"Oh, thanks, Hopie, but I just don't think I can concentrate enough right now to even listen to a book," he said.

It was the first time I felt truly scared for my dad.

Chapter 8

Back in California we didn't need to be taught about the melting pot of America. We lived it. The kids in my school pretty much represented the world. In Ohio the only thing melting is the snow, or so I hear. I remember as a kid thinking how strange it was that the US is broken up into segments: West, Northwest, Midwest, East. Isn't it the UNITED States? Now that I've experienced both California and Ohio, though, I understand it.

In California, each of my classes was filled with kids of various shades of brown. Most were bilingual and many belonged to families practicing the cultures of their native countries. This was the norm. If you mixed us all together, allowing our skin to swirl into one unified color, it would look like a specialty coffee drink, a mocha or caramel macchiato.

Here in Ohio it seems that the blending process was reversed, somehow, and each of the various tones of brown remain huddled together, protecting each other from the elements.

Instead of rain: judgements. In place of snow: distrust. There are plenty of families here in Youngstown representing the colors of the world, but they are different, somehow, than those in California, where separateness didn't exist because the blending was inevitable. I'm not saying there wasn't racism or prejudice. There was. It almost seems like the salty ocean air scrubbed us clean of the worst of it, though, and we were left with only a few who fought against the cleansing. The "us versus them" mentality here in Ohio makes me wonder where I fit in. Fortunately, though, I'm already the odd-one-out because I'm "the girl whose dad is dying."

Milo is a whole different story. Even though we moved smack dab in the middle of his high school experience, his status as a leader has already been secured. Milo is a soccer player, and I don't mean a lousy soccer player, like Abby. He's a really excellent halfback, which, if you don't know soccer, involves a lot of running. He was elevated to co-captain in a months' time.

I've discovered that here in the Middle West, sports are held in high esteem. Great news for Milo. Not so terrific for me. There aren't many after school clubs for a head-in-the-clouds dreamer, creative-type like me who stinks at sports and only stuck with piano lessons for eight months before selling on eBay all of the Indigo Girls sheet music that I insisted I would learn to play beautifully in order to buy the *The Hunger Games* in paperback.

೮೧೦೪

Milo pulled in from soccer practice just in time to help me finish dinner, spaghetti with tuna.

"Ugh, what's that smell?" he asked, joining me in the kitchen, his own sweaty odor providing a strong contrast to the canned fish I had just twisted open with the hand-held can opener, cutting my finger on the lid in the process.

"It's tuna," I said as I ran water over my finger, watching the little red drops swirl around in the sink like a miniature whirlpool before being sucked down the drain. I asked Milo to grab a bandage for me.

He returned with a Hello Kitty variety. "What? It's all I could find," he said, as I gave him a look. He grabbed the box of pasta and started to dump it into the boiling water.

"Wait!" I shouted. "Wash your hands first and then break it in half before you put it in the water," I ordered.

"Geez, who put you in charge?" he asked, apparently annoyed at my desire to serve a nice dinner for our family.

"Look, you were gone and Mom isn't home yet. Dad's resting and I didn't want to wake him to cook us dinner. I'm capable of making pasta, Milo, and you're welcome to help, but we're going to make it my way," I said, challenging him a bit.

"OK, OK, I'll wash my hands," he said, walking to the sink to oblige me. "Do you require anything else, Your Highness?" he joked, immediately lightening the mood.

"No," I said, realizing how much he reminded me of Dad in that moment. "Actually, after you start the pasta you can cut up some strawberries. I want to have some fruit with dinner," I said.

"Oh yeah?" he asked. "You on a health kick?"

"No," I said, hesitating on whether to continue, then deciding that Milo could be trusted with my new information.

"I did some research on cancer and learned that certain foods were sometimes found to shrink tumors."

He stopped digging in the refrigerator and turned to look at me. "Let me guess. Tuna and strawberries?" he asked sarcastically.

"Yeah, so what?" I yelled. "How could it hurt, Milo? How could it hurt to try?"

He jerked his head back to look at me, as if my forceful words had pulled at him with an invisible string. "It couldn't," he shrugged in agreement. "It couldn't hurt to try."

Chapter 9

There's a beautiful boy in a few of my classes: Malik Anderson, who, because of alphabetical order, always sits up front, while I bring up the rear. Don't get me wrong, I like the way he looks, but I'm drawn to him because he's smart and funny and real. Not like the gaggle of girls who prance by my locker every morning wearing short skirts and shirts that give them the appearance of cleavage. The other thing I like about Malik? He doesn't seem much interested in those girls.

I've caught him glancing at me a few times, but I always look away, as if I were casually scanning the room, not looking to see if he was looking at me.

When Malik smiles, his eyes crinkle up and nearly disappear. It's as if his smile consumes his whole face, and all you can focus on are his beautiful white teeth.

Aside from that, though, when Malik smiles you can feel the confidence oozing from the core of his being. He likes himself. And I don't mean that he's cocky, just confident; an unusual trait to find in a seventh-grader.

Sometimes, when I practice my own smile in the mirror, I try and smile like Malik, my whole face involved, my eyes crinkled. Unfortunately I look like I've been attacked by aliens, who are pointing laser rays against my back and whispering in my ear: *smile and tell your friends that everything's just fine.* Yep, that's exactly how I look.

Malik, though, he is the real deal. I wish I could get to know him better, but (and this sounds really dumb, I know) I don't want anyone to get in the way of me and Dad right now. He needs to be my focus, not Malik.

Fortunately, though, I can sit in the back of class watching Malik and his friends from afar. I can watch him laugh and smile as Mr. Fallon asks the class who wants to be in charge of feeding our pet rats, Pepe and Le Pew. Everyone does, except me. I don't raise my hand, but I watch Malik raise his, then turn around and smile his amazing, squinty-eyed smile as he laughs along with the class.

Yes, watching Malik is something that I can definitely do right now.

ဆၣ

It was on the bus on the way home from school when it hit me. Somehow my thoughts about Malik's smile and cool confidence reminded me of this girl at my middle school back in California named Nadia. She was gorgeous and knew it. Hers was a cocky sort of confidence.

Nadia was taller than my mom, with dark brown eyes, long dark brown hair, and even longer legs. Maybe because everyone was intimidated by her striking looks, she didn't so much have friends as followers.

Nadia was a model who had even been in a couple of TV spots, including Gap and Old Navy, the exact audience of the kids at my school. Like I said, she was gorgeous. The boys adored her and she led them along like puppies on a leash, batting her eyes and asking them to carry her books. They always did.

I was always curious about Nadia. What was her home life like? What were her hopes and dreams? Did she want to have friends? I never got to know her very well.

"Nadia," I mouthed to myself as the bus rounded the corner into my neighborhood.

As I said it, I sat up a little straighter, assuming her confident air. Nadia represents independence, glamour, and new beginnings.

Besides, if I'm Nadia then she becomes Hope. And let's face it, her future does look bright.

Lord save us all from a hope tree that has lost the faculty of putting out blossoms.
-Mark Twain

PART II - *Winter*

Chapter 10

"Hello, dear Hope," Dr. Ellie said, sweeping me into her office with a one arm, while squeezing my hand with the other.

"Hey, guess what?" I offered excitedly, sitting in the rocking chair across from her.

"What?" she asked with a smile.

"I came up with a name! Just like you said, it came out of nowhere and hit me like a ton of bricks!" I shared.

"Is that what I said?" she asked, tilting her head a little to the side.

"Well, something like that," I said. "Anyway, I've decided on Nadia."

"Nadia," she repeated, lengthening each syllable and drawing the name out. "It's a beautiful name, Hope. Have you shared your decision with your parents?"

"No, not yet," I said. "I just came up with it at school on Monday and I wanted you to be the first to know," I offered like a gift, then immediately shifted gears.

"I've had the same dream three times now," I informed Dr. Ellie, almost proud of my mind's ability to focus in on one subject matter even while sleeping.

"Ah, the recurrent dream," said Dr. Ellie. "Would you like to share?"

"Yeah, but it's nothing very exciting," I said. "Just me and Dad goofing around in the woods, playing our game."

"Goofing around?" asked Dr. Ellie.

"Oh, just running around playing tag," I said. "Back in California, we had a wooded area behind our house and we would play tree tag for fun. You know, running from tree to tree, trying to avoid getting tagged." I giggled at the memory.

Dr. Ellie smiled at me. "Is it a funny game?"

"It's just that I'm pretty sure Dad let me win every time. He was always chasing me, never quite catching up. He must have looked so silly to the neighbors, running in slow motion trying to catch me."

I smiled, yet something was bothering me. It must have shown on my face.

"What changed just now, Hope?" Dr. Ellie leaned forward a bit, taking me in with her eyes.

"I, uh, I just realized that in this dream I was 'it'. That I was chasing him," I said aloud as the true memory of the dream came to me all at once. "He was ahead of me, and I couldn't see his face. I could never see his face," I said quietly, looking down at my hands.

It surprised me that I hadn't recognized this before I brought up the dream. When I woke up this morning, it was with the feeling that I had experienced déjà vu. A memory of a past event. Now I realized that the game had changed. This was a new experience; Dad had a destination and I wasn't invited. The sense of the dream was that Dad

48

was trying to shake me, keep me from him.

I glanced at Dr. Ellie and saw her concern.

"Hope, I wonder if you would like to tell me what you think your dream is about."

I shrugged, then offered, "Why wouldn't he want me to be there?"

"Where, Hope?" she asked. "Where does your dad not want you to be?"

"In the woods. Out in the woods. I can handle the woods," I said a bit lounder than I intended. "There's nothing out there I can't handle!" I boomed at her.

There was a lengthy pause as Dr. Ellie considered what I had just shouted at her. The silence was just beginning to make me squirm when she quietly asked, "What about Nadia? Is there something Nadia can handle that Hope cannot?"

I didn't answer her. I didn't answer myself. It was a question for which there seemed to be no answer, only the lack of an answer. The lack of an answer motivated me, however, to hop right up, grab my bag and head for the door. Dr. Ellie did not call to me, did not follow me. I left the door open and strolled right out of her office, to where the sun was shining on my face, quickly drying the tears that had collected at the corners of my eyes. Dad was sitting in the car, reading his *Newsweek*. I took a breath, smiled, and climbed into the passenger seat.

"That was quick," he said.

"Yeah, Dr. Ellie had a client with an emergency and had to cut our session short," I said, lying to my dad. "I'm sure she'll still charge you the same rate, though," I joked.

Dad laughed, teasing "I'm sure she's getting her money's worth with you anyway."

I smiled back at Dad and turned to look at myself in the car's side mirror, ignoring the truth I had injected into my lie.

49

Chapter 11

I went with Dad to his chemo appointment for the first time today. I pretended to be cavalier about it, but the stark reality hit me when we arrived at the doctor's office. The receptionist was very friendly as my dad introduced me to her. I wasn't sure that I liked how he spoke to this woman in such a familiar way, as if he had been spending all this social time with her. I suppose he had, though, with chemo treatments once a week.

She asked about Milo, too, and Mom, then asked us to take a seat, that the nurse would call us back in a few minutes.

"*Time* or *Newsweek*?" Dad asked with a grin, holding the most recent edition of each in his hands. He was teasing me, knowing how I enjoyed catching up on the latest Hollywood gossip with *People* whenever I went to the doctor or dentist.

"Why don't you stick with world news, Dad, while I catch up on J.Lo's twins," I said, elbowing him in the arm. He really was the best.

We both quickly became absorbed in our rags – I in the most recent love triangle between Jennifer, Brad, and Angelina (Branjenlina), and Dad in the plight of women living in fear in Afghanistan. "It's such a violation of human rights," he said, mostly to himself, as he read the story of a woman being arrested for driving. "Driving!" he mocked. "Oh the horror!"

I held on tight to my *People*, but listened closely, Dad's commentary reminding me of his passionate interest in all things just.

"John, come on back," called the nurse, interrupting our moment.

"Hello again, Robin," Dad said with a smile. "Glad to see me?"

The nurse smiled back. "I bet this is Hope," she said. "She's a spitting image of you – in a really pretty package."

"Hmm, I don't know if I should be insulted or honored," Dad joked back.

"Actually, it's Nadia," I said, testing out my name for the first time, liking the way it rolled off my tongue.

Dad raised his eyebrows.

"Okay, well hi, Nadia," said Robin-The-Nurse, holding the door open with her petite frame. "You know the drill, John. Room three is on your left."

"Hi," I said back, though they had already moved on down the hall.

"Nadia, you can bring the magazine along, if you want. This will take a good hour or so," Robin-The-Nurse said.

"Oh, OK," I said, turning back to retrieve my magazine.

Dad was sitting in a chair when I met up with them in Room 3. Robin-The-Nurse was taking his blood pressure. "170/84," she said, "a little high. Have you been checking it at home?"

"It's been hovering around 150/70," Dad said. "Probably just nervous about the big needle headed my way," he said, winking at me.

"Well, be sure to keep checking it. We want to make sure it doesn't stay elevated. How's your appetite been? I see you've lost five more pounds since last week."

My dad sighed, "Either this is the best diet I've ever been on, or I'm working toward the lightweight category." Dad and his jokes.

"I know the chemo can make you nauseous, but it's so important to keep up your strength. Have you tried the supplemental shakes like we discussed?"

"Not yet," Dad said. "I was hoping it would level off by now. We'll pick some up on the way home."

"Good. You should continue to aim for two thousand calories per day. You can supplement with liquids if chewing makes you too nauseous."

I picked up my *People* and turned to a page I had noticed earlier with yet another bony-thin celebrity staring out at me with her pronounced collarbones and scrawny arms. I wondered if she had suffered to be so skinny. In her quest for thin, had she too become adverse to chewing?

"Do you have any questions for me, John?" Robin The Nurse asked.

"Nope, I think we're good to go, right honey?" Dad said.

"Yep, good to go," I said. And I really wished I could be going, but we were just getting started.

Dad was sent to another larger room with a reclining chair and several machines. He rolled up the sleeve on his left arm and lay back, closing his eyes as if he were preparing for a spa treatment, the kind where they place cucumber rounds over your eyes while smearing the rest of your face with an avocado spread.

He looked relaxed, and I was envious of his ability to lie there zoning out the stark white walls and sharp ammonia smell that made this room so unappealing.

There was a gentle knock on the door and Dad's doctor entered the room with Dad's file in hand.

"Hello, John," he said, reaching out his hand for an obligatory handshake.

"Dr. Phillips, this is my daughter, Hope," Dad said, introducing me to the man who was about to inject my dad with enough poison to kill cells in his body. Hopefully the right cells.

"Nice to meet you," I said, "but please call me Nadia," I said, sitting up straighter.

"Hello, Nadia," he said glancing at my dad. "Did you see that they picked the next contestants on 'Dancing with the Stars'?" he asked, nodding to the magazine I had placed on the table beside me.

"Uh, no, I haven't read the whole thing yet," I said. "Anyone good?"

"Do you like football?" he asked.

"Not really," I said.

"Well, then you may not be as interested," he said.

What I was interested in was that my dad's oncologist was taking the time to read *People* magazine and watching 'Dancing with the Stars' when my dad was sick. Where were his priorities?

"I hear you still don't have much of an appetite," Dr. Phillips said to Dad.

"No, but Robin gave me the evil eye. I'll take care of it," Dad said with a grin.

"Good idea," said Dr. Phillips. "You definitely don't want to get on Robin's bad side."

As he was talking, Dr. Phillips was rubbing my dad's arm down with an alcohol swab, preparing it for the needle stick of the I.V. I watched as he stuck it into my dad's vein, without flinching, though I noticed Dad looking away in the final seconds. I probably would have done the same if it had been my arm.

"Okay, John, the hard part's over," Dr. Phillips said. "I'm going to start the drip. Remember, you might feel a burning sensation followed by a cold sensation as it moves into your bloodstream. You should be all set in about thirty minutes, but Robin will stop in to check on you in a little bit. Do you need anything?"

"Hope, honey," Dad said, "Dr. Phillips is asking you a question."

"Sorry," I said, realizing I had zoned out, letting the name slide this time.

"Do you need anything? A Coke or lemonade?" asked Dr. Phillips.

"Oh, no thank you," I said. I couldn't bear the thought of drinking a sweet treat while Dad sat next to me with poison dripping into his shrinking body.

"I'm just going to catch up on 'Dancing with the Stars,'" I said, holding up the magazine.

"Let me know what you think," said Dr. Phillips, more than likely speaking of the celebrities chosen for the show.

I didn't have the guts to tell him what I thought about his primeval plan to cure my dad of cancer. The truth was, I thought it sucked. Dad, on the other hand, was lying back, eyes closed, and in relaxation pose. I didn't understand how he was doing it.

℥℺

The next day, Dad didn't join us for breakfast.

"Where is he?" I asked Mom, who was busy throwing together a lunch for her day.

"He's not feeling well," she said. "He had his chemo yesterday, and is feeling pretty nauseated."

"I was there, remember?" I said, not very kindly.

"Right, you went with him," she said, shuffling through the fruit drawer in the refrigerator, past the moldy strawberries. "Damn, I thought I bought some apples," she muttered to herself.

"They're on the other side," I said, pointing to the vegetable drawer.

She turned around to look at me. "If you noticed them in the wrong drawer, why didn't you move them?" she asked.

"Geez, and a good morning to you too! I didn't even have to tell you!" I yelled, slamming my spoon down on the table and leaving my half-eaten bowl of Cheerios to become a soggy mess. I stomped upstairs and slammed my door, locking it behind me.

She just doesn't get it, she just doesn't get it, she just doesn't get it, ran through my head over and over like a mantra that I had been saying so often lately it created a relaxed and meditative quality. I sat on my bed with my journal and picked up a pen to write down the words that I dared not scream out loud to my mom when there was a knock at my bedroom door.

"I don't want to talk to you!" I yelled through the hollow wooden barricade separating me from Mom.

"It's Dad," said the voice on the other side.

"Oh, sorry," I said, jumping up to open the door. "Sorry, I thought it was, well, I just needed some privacy," I said.

He looked terrible. His skin so pale it looked blue, especially the area under his eyes, which were bloodshot. His arms were covered in little pink dots.

"What is wrong with your arms?" I asked, pointing to the tiny pinpricks all up the inside of each of his forearms.

"It's petechia. I've got a quality case of dry heaves," he said,

56

patting his stomach. "The good news is there's nothing much in here to come up."

"Dad, you should be in bed," I said, pointing to my own.

"I think I'll take you up on that," he said, moving slowly across the room to the edge of my bed. "Those stairs did me in."

"Hope," he said after a moment catching his breath. "Your mom needs you right now. You know that, don't you? Out of all of us, this," he said swooping his arm down his body, "has been hardest on her. Please give her a break once in a while. Please. Can you do that?

I sighed.

"If you can't do it for her sake, please just do it for my sake. I need you to be nicer to her. Give her a break," he said.

"I try, Dad, but she's so unreasonable right now," I said.

"I know. She's unreasonable. But so much in our lives is unreasonable right now. Reason has nothing to do with how we should treat each other, especially right now. Right now we need to be holding on, not pushing away. Does that make sense?" he asked.

"Yes," I said quietly. "But why does it have to be me? Why does she get to keep pushing and I have to hold on? It's not fair."

"It's not fair, that's true," Dad said, pushing the covers aside as he slipped his thin, pale body beneath them. "But it needs to be you, Hope. It just needs to be you. Trust me."

And I wanted to. I'd never had a reason not to trust my dad in my life, ever. I couldn't help but flinch, though, when I looked over and saw my mom standing in the doorway, blotting at her eyes with a tissue.

"Well, since I have you both in the same room, I want you to do something for me," I said, asserting myself. Then, before they could speak, "I want you to forget Hope and call me Nadia," I said.

"Nadia?" asked Mom.

57

"Yes, Nadia," I said annunciating the syllables.

"We can try, right Anna?" Dad asked. But Mom was gone.

Chapter 12

Now that I had my new name all worked out, I was more determined than ever to get to court and become Nadia. I was still faced with the obstacle of the unsigned guardian papers, but I was working on that.

Every night I placed my papers under Dad's pillow. My notes to him were now a daily occurrence, and focused entirely on persuading him to sign. I listed good and valid reasons: "I'll still look the same," and "You never asked my opinion about being Hope in the first place." I included the *National Geographic* article Dad had read to me about the tribe in Africa, which took some serious internet research to locate. I knew with Dad I would have to hit hard and hit often, presenting my case like a lawyer in front of a judge. I learned this last fall when I wanted so desperately to see Coldplay in concert.

My parents thought I was too young for concerts, but I knew better. I researched their song lyrics to show Dad that I wouldn't be corrupted by vulgarity. I showed him their website and we listened to "Viva la Vida," which I loved for the guitar rift, and "Fix You," which I learned Chris Martin had written for his wife, Gwyneth Paltrow, after her father had died.

Even though this was months before Dad's cancer diagnosis, that bit of information seemed to resonate with him, and we ended up going to the concert together, along with Milo. It rocked, it rolled, and was all-around awesome! I did catch a whiff of marijuana floating around, which I had never smelled before that night, but its pungent, earthy aroma was unmistakable, leaving me feeling light and airy. I will forever associate that smell with my dad reaching out to grab hold of my hand, smiling at me with a look of adoration while Coldplay blew our minds with their live version of the song I had used in my closing argument.

For now, though, the work at hand was convincing my dad to sign my papers, and coming up with the money to pay for my court costs. They weren't cheap and I was too young to get a real job. I would have to take what I could get, which meant Henry. The three year-old terror.

"Hi Aunt Susan," I said into the receiver. "It's Hope. Yep, he's fine. Yes, I'm sure." *Geez.* "Anyway, I wanted to let you know that I'm available to watch Henry for you after school sometimes. Uh-huh. Yeah? Sure, I can do that. Um, I bet Milo could drop me off. Okay, see you tomorrow."

Well, that was easy. I had no idea how desperate parents were to get out of the house. Actually, Aunt Susan said that Lily's dance classes and cheer competitions kept her and Uncle Dave very busy, and it wasn't any fun to chase Henry around the bleachers for three hours at a time. I was hired, starting tomorrow.

Henry made me work for my five dollars an hour, let me tell you! I was so exhausted after the first evening that I crawled into bed and turned the light out without reading. The only other time I remember not reading myself to sleep was on a camping trip with the family two years ago. Mom thought Dad had packed the lantern and vice versa. We had to get by with the light of the campfire and I didn't want to take the chance of *Little Women* being scorched by flecks of burning embers as they popped up into the air and landed, still glowing, on anything in their path.

Henry reminded me of those little prickles of heat, which fell upon my legs that night around the fire. He burned me up with his tyrannical ways, and it wasn't long before my true nature came out, Henry my unassuming victim. I wish that I felt ashamed of what I did, but I honestly don't. It felt good, and the best part is that only I will ever know my dirty little secret.

When I showed up to babysit, Lily was dressed in her cheer uniform, with its short, perky purple and white striped skirt and deep V-neck purple tank top. The symbol of a yellow sunburst shone happily on the front. Lily was fully made up, with mascara curling her perfect eyelashes so that they looked just like the models on those lash-enhancing commercials. Each lash separated and elongated. She had rosy, blush-covered cheeks; pink, glossy lips; and dark blue eyeshadow, exaggerating the bright blue eyes she came by naturally. Her golden hair was pulled up into a high ponytail and curled in little springy sections. She looked adorable and perfect. All she needed was a dab of Vaseline on her teeth to keep her smile from drying out.

That image was burned into my mind as I sat on the floor with Lily's terror of a brother, playing cars versus dinosaurs on the carpet. My red Mustang was no competition against a T-Rex. Henry pounced, pummeling both my car and hand with his oversized lizard. I was being preyed upon by a three year-old while my thirteen year-old cousin was having the time of her life in purple and white.

Dinnertime rolled around and I took Henry into the kitchen with me as I read Aunt Susan's note:

Mac-n-Cheese and green beans in the pantry. Henry will eat the beans right out of the can, no need to heat up. Please feed Bess a can of dog food (in the garage). She likes 'Filet Mignon' best.

Don't we all?

It wasn't even a conscious decision, but as I was stirring up the butter, milk, and powdered cheese into the macaroni, I added a spoonful of Bess' dinner into the pot. I mixed and stirred until the chunky brown dollop became incorporated into the nearly fluorescent orange dish I had prepared for Henry. He ate without complaint, asking for "More, more!" When he finished, I spooned the remaining macaroni into a plastic container, leaving the rest of the family vulnerable to my mean streak. I held my hunger at bay, waiting until I got home to devour some leftover pepperoni pizza straight from the box.

It just seemed fair, the Coopers eating dog food. They would never know and I would never tell them. Their perfect little family would continue to operate under that illusion, but I would know better. They might never need to learn the side effects of chemo or need to talk to a therapist, God-forbid, but they will have consumed Bess' favorite filet mignon.

Fortunately for me, the garage was stacked with it.

ॐ

11/29

Dear Nadia,

You've had quite a week, haven't you? Who are you, anyway? Hope was such a sweet, dutiful girl, and you just do whatever pops in your mind. I kind of like it, though. Next thing you know you'll be holding up banks in a tight black bodysuit, taking off with bags of money, living in a tropical paradise, just like in the movies. Do you think banks even have bags of money anymore? Nobody uses cash much these days. Everything just lives on the computer. Well, maybe you'll become a computer hacker!

One thing's for sure. I like you, Nadia. Better than that flaky old Hope.

Love, Me

Chapter 13

It was Mom's idea that she and I take a photography class together. Well, not photography specifically, but find a hobby that we could enjoy together. I know Mom is trying to figure out a way to connect with me, but I doubt that an hour a week taking pictures will work that kind of magic. I can't exactly say no, can I? I mean, Mom needs this. She must, because she's never asked anything of me before.

The local art center offers a few different options for expressing one's creativity: knitting, cooking, ceramics, and photography. Apparently Grandma tried to teach Mom to knit many years ago, but she spent more time untangling the skeins of yarn than learning any useful garment-making skills.

Cooking was out too. The last time Mom "cooked," she caught the oven on fire trying to broil homemade tortilla chips. Those chips lit up like they had been sprayed with gasoline! She managed to grab the pot-holders, yank the cookie sheet out of the inferno, and throw the whole mess into the sink, turning the water on full-blast. The fire was contained, but every one of our downstairs smoke detectors started screaming, and the entire house smelled of burnt food for several days. All for chips and salsa. The last time I checked, tortilla chips cost two bucks at the grocery.

Ceramics made mom think of ashtrays, which reminded her of smoking, which led to a full-blown anxiety attack remembering that her husband was dying of lung cancer. It was out too.

Photography it was.

The first thing we did was head to Mac's Camera for a look at the newest models. Who knew photography could be such an expensive hobby? Four hundred dollars later, we were armed with the latest in digital technology. Our camera did it all: custom settings for all types of environments, twelve times zoom lens, with panoramic settings, black and white, and, of course, red-eye reduction.

Our class met on Tuesday nights from seven to nine. The instructor was Lewis MacConley, himself, the owner of Mac's Camera. At the first class, he brought dozens of samples of his work for us to see. I especially loved the pictures he took of angels. I asked him about it and he told me that he visits cemeteries in his search for the perfect limestone angel. He particularly likes finding angels with a large tree nearby. "The sun and shadow created from the leaves adds dramatic lighting," he said.

Maybe we'll get Dad an angel for his gravestone. I would love to have an L. Mac original of my dad someday.

I discovered that my style of photography was finding something quirky in the everyday ordinary. For example, I got a great picture of a farmer up on his tractor talking on his cell phone. I have no clue how he could hear anything over the engine, but it made for an interesting shot.

I also love the photo I got of the big Methodist Church downtown the day after someone ironically spray painted "I ♥ Dog" on the building. I'm not saying I condone that sort of thing, but it did make for a great picture. Mac agreed, gushing over my "great eye for detail," my ability to "pick out what others miss." He encouraged me to sign up for his advanced class, which included darkroom privileges. I told him I would consider it, until I realized the real reason Mom wanted me to take photography classes with her.

I wasn't initially concerned when my mom began taking pictures only of me. I get the whole mother's pride thing, but I was her singular focus. I should have known she was up to something. I saw the progression of pictures each week. I suffered through the humiliation of the class viewing picture after picture of me. One even showed me with a huge bite of scrambled egg in my mouth, wearing my ratty old "Sea You Later" mermaid t-shirt, my hair a mess!

The final straw, though, was the picture Mom took of me, all pumped up at Milo's soccer game. I remember the scene well: the score was tied, one all, and Milo was dribbling the ball down the field, cutting to the left past the first defender, then to the right to open up his shot. In a matter of seconds, the ball went arching through the air to land in the goalie's "blind spot," the upper left corner of the goal.

I also remember, in the excitement of the moment, turning to my dad for our usual celebratory high-five. What I didn't recall was the flash of a bulb, forever burning that image onto a now eight by ten sheet, presented to our photography class with the title "My Hope."

The class oohed and aahed over the jubilation captured in mine and my dad's faces and L. Mac congratulated my mom on finding her inner voice. I sat back and fumed. I had been duped once again. My mom had discovered my weak spot and had taken full advantage of it. I had let my guard down and I was determined not to let it happen again.

Photography class had lasted three weeks and I was to be its first casualty.

ഇാരു

December 15

Hopie,

It's getting cold, isn't it? I don't know if it's because I'm so thin right now (back to my college weight at last!), or if it's been so long since I've experienced winter, but I am chilled to the bone these days.

Remember when we had that cold snap in California a couple of years ago? You seemed so little then and were convinced that we would have snow. You begged us to take you to the store to buy a sled — I wasn't even sure they sold sleds in California — but we took you anyway. You were so mad by the time we hit the fourth store that you marched right up to the customer service desk and asked to see the manager. There was no stopping you, Hope. Still isn't. You are so determined to have your way and I marvel at your maturity to get what you need. I don't think I stood up for myself until halfway through my thirties. You, though, were born with this instinct.

I know I've said this before, but please try to contain your instinct to take your frustration out on your mother. She is a little lost right now and needs our support. She's trying, Hope, she's trying her best to be who I need her to be right now. I think we all just need to cut her a little slack.

I love you, Dad

Chapter 14

Mr. Fallon did not appreciate my humor in science class this morning. He did not find it funny, for instance, when I raised my hand during class to dispute the textbook's claims about risk-taking behaviors. I simply made the (valid) point that, hey, we're all gonna die someday, just like my dad, so why not live life to the extreme: smoke, skydive, get a tattoo or seven. He asked me to stay after class.

My cheeks burned as I watched my classmates file out the door after the period bell.

"Hope," he said, "I understand what you're going through. I lost my mom to cancer last year. It was hard to watch her suffer through so much pain." He looked at me with that look I knew well: pity.

He described the long nights in the hospital and the painful reality of her passing.

"The thing is, Hope, you can't expect these kids," he said, sweeping his arm out beyond the halls, "to relate to you when you bring up the personal details. You want to make some friends, don't you? Meet a couple of girls that you can hang out with when you need to escape. You have to meet them at their level, which is pretty self-absorbed."

I must say, I was a little shocked to hear a teacher say that out loud, but it must not have registered on my face because he kept going on about the ways I could fit in.

Finally, he was finished. I knew because he put his hand on my shoulder and nearly shoved me out the door.

"Let me know if you ever want to talk again, Hope. My door is always open," Mr. Fallon said with a smile.

I smiled back, nodding my head in understanding, all the while thinking to myself that I had not uttered a word during "our" talk. As far as I was concerned, Mr. Fallon was the one self-absorbed enough to fit in perfectly with the students he just described. I ran to make it to Spanish on time, collecting warnings from Ms. Haynes and Mr. Plummer, as I did.

I was exhausted when I got home. Physically and emotionally. I felt completely misunderstood and more alone than ever.

Mom had left me a note on the table: *Made some banana bread. Letter from Abby in the front room.* I raced to the living room and found the blue envelope on top of the stack of mail.

I just talked to Abby last Thursday on her birthday. She had called on her new cell phone and given me a hard time about not joining Facebook, but social networking seemed like a slap in my dad's face.

"Pretty please!" Abby begged. "It'll be so much easier to keep up with each other."

And she was right, it would be easier. But I didn't care. I didn't want to manage a profile that dared open up the pity party for the whole world to participate.

"Fine, we'll just write letters, like pioneers," Abby joked. She was my best friend in the whole world and understood me better than anyone, besides Dad, maybe.

I picked up the letter and tore it open as I walked back towards the kitchen to slice a piece of my mom's bread offering.

Nadia,

How cool is it that you're changing your name! It sounds perfect for you - kinda exotic, don't you think? I miss you tons and hope Ohio is treating you well. Have you met any fun girls? Cute boys? I have the biggest crush on Landon. I know, I know, he was always really goofy with that curly red hair, but now I think it's kind of cute.

Since you refuse to join the 21st century and join Facebook, as soon as I can come up with the money I'm going to add texting so we can keep in touch even better.

I rolled my eyes at that one, considering I also don't have a cell phone. Who's she going to text? My brother, to pass along the message?

We all miss you, especially me and Grover (Abby's cat). *I'll call you soon and we can catch up on everything.*

Your BFF,
Jasmine
(I decided if you were going to change your name, I would too. I've always wanted a more exotic-sounding name!)
I shook my head in disgust. *Oh, Abby, you of all people?*

71

Turns out I'm still misunderstood.

୫୦ଓଃ

I expected Dr. Ellie to berate me right off the bat for the way our last session ended. I had avoided her for a month, making excuses to my parents as to why I couldn't make my therapy sessions. For as much time as I spent on "school projects" in the past month, they were definitely expecting straight A's.

Instead, Dr. Ellie greeted me with a warm welcome, as she typically did, and sat down in her white chair. I sat on the couch, on the end nearest her, close enough to observe the details of her beautiful necklace, swirling with silver, orange, and red. It looked great with her brown sweater. I quietly complimented her.

"Thanks! It's great to see you, Hope," she said with a smile.

Our agreement had been for her to continue calling me Hope until Nadia is my official, legal name. I'm sure there is a psychological reason for her insistence of this, and although I feel it's time to renegotiate the terms of this agreement, I simply feel relieved that she is still speaking to me after my behavior at our last session.

"You too," I say softly, glancing at her shyly, through eyes pointed to the floor but looking up at hers.

"Hope, you look positively ashamed," she said, with a hint of amusement. "Are you recalling our last session?"

"I'm sorry I ran out," I admitted. "I just needed some space."

"Absolutely understandable," she said. "Apology accepted. How have you been?" she asked, moving forward at the speed of light.

I realize that I love this about Dr. Ellie. With anybody else, an accepted apology is simply the beginning of the forgiveness process. Feelings are hurt and linger, the situation is brought up time and time again as an example of "what not to do." It feels great to be forgiven and trust that my outburst and subsequent flight will not be thrown back in my face. I decide to take note of this and store it away for future use.

"It's been fine. Dad's chemo is almost finished, I think two more rounds. He feels better, or at least he's not sick all the time anymore. Mom has been working more too, so she must feel the same way. Before last week she was hanging around the house a lot, fussing after Dad. I think we're all pretty sure the chemo is working. Everyone just seems to be back to normal. Whatever that means, right?" I joked, shifting my shoulders up, rolling my eyes and grinning at Dr. Ellie, who was scribbling something down on her notepad.

She finished her writing and looked up at me, very somber. It scared me a little.

"Hope, I want to spend a little time on the stages of grief today," she said, taking off her glasses and setting them on the table next to her, trading them for her handy box of tissues, which she set down on the coffee table in front of us.

As she talked about denial, anger, bargaining, depression, I nodded politely, pretending to be engaged in the conversation. Yes, I could recognize most of these in my thoughts and behaviors, but I really didn't care.

What *does* really freak me out is acceptance. I mean, really, how can I ever accept losing my dad? I wanted to ask Dr. Ellie if acceptance was a stage you only reached in your last fifteen minutes of life on earth, but didn't.

How can I, a girl with a ridiculously ironic name, ever accept losing my dad?

"Dr. Ellie," I said, interrupting her as she dug through her bookcase, looking for some book she thought might help me understand my grieving process.

"Yes?" she asked, still hunched over, turning her head to look at me.

"You do know that Dad's not really my problem right now, right?" I asked, quite convinced.

"He's not?" she asked, making her way back to the couch to sit on the end opposite me, facing me with her left leg pulled up under her right.

"Nope. Mom," I said, reduced to one-word sentences.

Dr. Ellie said nothing, leaving it up to me to continue the conversation I now regretted even bringing up.

"Mom," I said again. "You know? The woman in my life."

"I know who you mean, Hope, but I'd like to know why your mother is your problem right now," she said.

"She keeps butting into my life, trying to 'connect' with me," I said making quotations with my fingers to clarify the word. "I just wish she'd leave me alone and let me spend time with Dad."

"You feel as if your mother is getting in the way of your relationship with your father?" Dr. Ellie asked, her eyes never leaving mine.

"I guess so," I said.

"Please, Hope, keep going. I like how well you are expressing yourself today," she encouraged.

I took the bait.

"Yeah, I mean Dad and I, we used to be a team. And I liked it, just the two of us. Well, sometimes Milo too, and then it was the three of us. And that worked too. Mom got to do what she loved and so did we," I told her. "But then when we moved here and everything changed. Mom is so needy all the time and just expects me to be there for her, even though," I stopped, looking down at my hands, which were gripping one of Dr. Ellie's intricately-embroidered pillows like a vice.

"Even though?" Dr. Ellie repeated.

"I don't know," I said, stopping myself. "She just drives me crazy."

"Hope, would you please stand up with me?" Dr. Ellie asked, reaching out a hand.

"Okay," I said, though I hesitated.

She smiled. "I promise we aren't going to dance."

I stood, facing Dr. Ellie.

"Sometimes a little change of scenery helps," she said, walking to the door, opening it for me. "Your mom is driving you crazy. She's needy, right?"

I nodded, walking out into the hall, following her outside, onto the front steps.

"Hope, I wonder if your mom is simply trying to figure out a way to join the team," she said, shielding her eyes from the sun.

I shrugged. "Maybe."

"It's tough being picked last," she said, waving to my dad, who had pulled up alongside the building.

"Will you think about it?" she asked. "Perhaps write about it in your journal?"

I shrugged a second time and headed off to hang out with my team.

Chapter 15

I listened to my parents in the vent again this morning. I knew it was worth listening to when they were so loud I could hear them through the hum of my hair dryer.

"I don't care what Dr. Ellie says, we're not giving in to her!" Mom said forcefully.

"Anna, it's not a matter of giving in, it's to help give Hope a feeling of control over all of this," my dad responded.

"Oh, and you think granting my daughter permission to go and *legally* change her name, the name you and I personally picked out, need I remind you, is going to give her a feeling of control?" Mom yelled.

"Well, yes, I guess I do," Dad said.

"You're crazy!" Mom yelled. "I don't know what's gotten into you lately! Maybe it's the chemo, or maybe it's because you have so much time on your hands, but..."

Silence.

Mom's words bounced around in my head, filling me with anger. I clenched my teeth and ducked my head closer to the vent.

"John, I'm so sorry," she said, choking on her words.

"Listen, Anna. I'm not thrilled to think about Hope changing her name either," he said, ignoring her apology, "but think about it in a different way, will you? Maybe if we just give a little on Hope's end, she will ease up on thinking she needs to involve the courts. What harm is there in calling her Nadia? Honestly, honey, we've been trying to get her head out of the clouds for years, and she seems really focused on making this happen. Why not give her some space?"

"God, what will the family think?" Mom asked, still sniffing.

"Who cares?" Dad said. "They'll probably think we're all crazy, but you know what? Maybe we are a little crazy. I know I am. Besides, Dr. Ellie seems the best judge of that in our lives right now, and she recommends allowing Hope some space to process all of this. It was her idea to…"

"I know, I know," Mom sighed, "she thinks we should call her Nadia."

I must have changed Dr. Ellie's mind yesterday, I thought, feeling powerful.

"Well, what could it hurt?" Dad said. "The way I figure it, the more we push back, the more she's going to want it. Remember Milo and the ferret?" Dad said.

I don't know about Mom, but I sure did.

About five years ago, Milo tried to convince Mom and Dad that he just *had* to have a ferret. His friend Tate got one for his birthday, and Milo was obsessed with him (the ferret, not Tate, though one might think so with as much time as Milo spent at his house playing with the ferret).

Anyway, Mom and Dad had no interest in having a ferret for a pet, but Milo was persistant. He finally wore them down. Two months later, Milo had saved enough to buy a ferret, which he did at his earliest opportunity. "That cage," the salesperson explained, "is escape-proof. As long as you lock the mechanism, your new little buddy won't be able to get out."

Either Milo didn't listen or he bought a mensa ferret, because that night, while Milo was sleeping, Tigger (the ferret), did escape and also managed to seek out a warm, dark spot to hide: under Milo's sheets. With Milo.

He screamed so loud at two in the morning that we heard the neighbor's dog start barking. Dad went running into the bedroom to find Milo hiding in the closet, while Dad was left to pull a spooked Tigger out of hiding and back into his escape-proof cage.

Tigger went back to the store the next day and Milo never mentioned ferrets again.

But if Dad thinks that's what's going to happen to Nadia after I've had a chance to write it on my school notebooks, he's got another thing coming. Because I am determined to change my name, legally, no matter what Mom or Dad or Dr. Ellie say.

Fortunately for me, based on the conversation in the vents, it sure sounds like I'm getting closer to reaching my goal.

ഇൻൽ

I didn't sleep well last night. I kept having that stupid dream about the woods. I would wake up in a panic, wondering where my dad had run off to, fall asleep, and wake up again as if someone had pressed 'pause' on a remote control out of my reach.

I woke up a little after five, a good hour and a half before my alarm was set to go off, tired of fighting a good night's sleep that was unlikely to happen.

I grabbed my robe and attempted to quietly open my bedroom door. The creaking was worse the slower I opened it, so, like ripping off a bandage, I flung the door open with one quick burst of sound. I didn't want to wake anyone else up. I wanted to be alone.

I headed downstairs to the living room and pressed the knob on the gas fireplace for a satisfying "whoosh" of blue flame, followed by the slight aroma of gas. I walked over to the front window, which was all fogged up, partly due to the forty degree difference in temperature between the outside and inside, but also because the seal was torn in spots, caulk hanging down like ribbons along the edges.

I used my hand to wipe clear a circle of condensation and looked outside. The light across the street illuminated a white world, and snow was falling fast. It was beautiful. It wasn't the first time I had seen snow – we had visited Ohio over Christmas break many times – but it was the first time I had experienced untouched snow. The plow had yet to come down the road, so there were no piles of dirty grey snow along the sides of the road. There were no tire tracks. No footprints. I could make out what looked like rabbit tracks along the front yard, but no rabbit was in sight.

I walked to the coat closet and grabbed my dad's down parka, a holdover from his college days, which we kept for just such occasions. Its navy blue quilted exterior was cool to the touch, but once the coat was on over my pajamas, I felt toasty warm. I hunted for a hat and gloves, finding a pair of Mom's in a cardboard box. I walked to the kitchen to grab the flashlight under the sink and headed outdoors.

The snow only came up to my ankles, but it was snowing so hard that I thought it could be knee-high by breakfast. The air was like a cold blast to my cheeks, which was the only part of my body unprotected, aside from my insides. My lungs burned with the first few inhalations, but adjusted to the temperature quickly.

It was a soft snow, not good for packing snowballs or snowpeople, but it made it easy to walk around. I hiked the perimeter of the yard, marking my territory with boot prints. The glow of the flashlight fell a few feet in front of me, guiding my way.

As I reached the back yard, I flashed the light up into the big oak tree and caught sight of a squirrel, temporarily frozen by my light, then scurrying up into the branches, out of my view.

I walked over to the tree and lay down on the ground, staring up into its bare, snow-covered branches. It was quiet down here on the ground, the wind less prominent. I remembered to put my hands up above my head and swipe them, along with my legs, a few time along the ground to make a snow angel.

I wondered how I might preserve this figure as I attempted to stand up, thinking carefully as I sat up, bringing my knees to my chest. I stood up where the angel's dress was flared out and hopped a foot away to take a look at my snowy creation.

From my vantage point under the oak tree, my angel of Hope looked beautiful, glistening in the white snow as my flashlight illuminated her perfectly.

Chapter 16

It must have been the cinnamon pinecones that Grandma dropped off last night, but I had a hard time sleeping in anticipation of Christmas morning. Don't get me wrong, I'm perfectly aware of the Santa ruse, have been for a few years. But there's just something magical about Christmas morning.

Maybe it's the anticipation of opening all of those shiny, ribboned packages that lay in neat piles under the tree. Maybe it's the understanding that Milo and I have a cease-fire just this one day each year. Maybe it's the homemade tea rings and hot cocoa. Maybe it's curiosity. What will I unwrap this year? What will Mom think of the beaded necklace I painstakenly made with the tiniest seed beeds, closing my eyes each time I reached into the pile so as to avoid the perfectly symmetrical colors I was so tempted to string together.

Maybe I just wanted to get it out of the way.

Christmas is the one day out of the year that makes me feel

spiritual. When I was a kid, I would pour over the huge white Bible that mom had inherited from her grandmother. Its pages were dog-eared, many of its passages underlined. I loved the way it smelled, like an old library, all condensed into one five-pound book. I loved looking at the pages in the middle, the story of Christ laid out in full-color illustrations.

I was especially drawn to the photo of Jesus on the cross, his hands and feet nailed in place, blood dripping down. His head adorned with a crown of thorns, more blood falling into his eyes.

I woke up before Milo one year, knowing that I wasn't allowed to open any presents before everyone was up. I crept into the family room and plugged in the tree, staring at its lit branches, my eye catching the angel on top. It reminded me of Jesus. I went to the bookshelf and pulled the big Bible off the shelf, opening it up to the illustration that mesmerized me: Jesus on the cross.

Even though it was Christmas, the celebration of Jesus' birth, I understood that his birth would come to mean his death. And that His death meant a birth for those who believed. At the ripe old age of eight, I had figured out the cycle of life one Christmas morning while paging through my great-grandmother's Bible.

I looked for the Bible now, but knew that it was still packed away in a moving box, stored in Grandma's attic, along with a great many other books we had yet to unpack. I closed my eyes and thought of the picture, but could only imagine my dad's face attached to that lean body, mortally wounded upon the cross.

I opened my eyes to find Milo stretching in the kitchen.

"Merry Christmas," he said with a yawn.

"Hi Milo, Merry Christmas," I said back.

"Want some cocoa?" he asked, reaching for the mugs.

"Sure," I said. "Hey, what do you think this is?" I asked, holding up an awkwardly-wrapped present in the obvious shape of a golf club.

He laughed. "I guess I made it on the 'nice' list again this year," he joked.

"Yeah, I guess so," I said understanding the inside joke.

One year Milo had been furious with me for defacing his Star Wars poster. I drew a little pencil moustache on Yoda's face – no big deal, right? But when he confronted me and I tried to erase it, most of the ink came off, leaving the little green guru with a permanent white moustache instead.

Milo got his revenge by writing me a note signed, "Santa," in which he informed me that, due to my antics, I had officially been taken off the 'nice' list and was doomed to be permanently moved to the 'naughty' list unless I changed my evil ways. He must have been in cahoots with my parents, because I specifically remember doing all of my chores without complaint for a good two weeks before Milo came clean and admitted his handiwork.

"Do you think we should wake up Mom and Dad?" I asked, as Milo brought me a piping hot mug of cocoa, straight from the microwave.

"Nah, let's let them sleep," he said, walking over to the TV and flipping through the channels until he found the "All Christmas, All the Time," channel, available the entire month of December.

"Rudolph?" he asked, handing me the remote.

"That's fine. It's a classic," I said, waving off his offer.

We settled in and watched as Rudolph came to appreciate his special uniqueness, making important contributions along the way.

༄༅

By the time Mom and Dad shuffled into the living room, Milo and

I had baked the tea rings, which had been rising overnight in the refrigerator. These individual cinnamon rolls were bound together by their ringed shape and gooey caramel icing.

I brewed a pot of coffee, one tablespoon of grounds per two cups, just like Dad taught me, allowing the aroma to fill the kitchen, sending its invisible yet powerful aromatic tendrils out into the other rooms of the house, beckoning my parents from the cozy confines of their bed.

"Good morning," they said groggily, reaching for their mugs. Mom had ordered "I Love Me" mugs out of a catalog last year, and, fortunately, they were among the boxes we unpacked when we moved into the rental house. I loved those mugs.

Milo set the table while I squeezed some oranges for fresh orange juice. We had six oranges which may sound like a lot, but, in reality, yielded something like a quarter cup of juice.

"Who's ready to unwrap some gitfts?" Dad asked, clapping his hands together, finally awake after two cups of coffee and a full belly.

"Me!" Milo and I cried out in unison, reverting back to childhood with the suggestion of presents.

We spread out around the tree in a semi-circle, Dad pulling up the rocking chair to sit on something more comfortable. Mom pulled up a pillow.

"Youngest goes first!" I called, keeping with tradition.

"Okay, Nadia, you first," said Dad, and I caught him winking at Mom.

I grabbed a large box covered in white wrapping paper with blue snowflakes. I shook it. Nothing.

I removed the bow to keep for our traditional bow garland, and tore off the paper. Inside the box was a set of owl pajamas. "Thanks!" I said, jumping up to give mom and dad a hug.

Milo went next, opening the awkwardly-wrapped golf club.

"Awesome!" he said. Mom left and came back with the rest of the set, which she had hidden away in the back of the coat closet.

"You might need these to actually play a game," she said, although she really wouldn't know, having never played a game of golf in her life.

"Thanks, guys!" said Milo, polishing the head of the club with his shirt until it shone.

"Anna?" said Dad, pointing to the tree. There was a small package wrapped beautifully, hidden among the branches.

"John!" said Mom, surprised. "I thought we decided not to exchange gifts this year," she argued as she reached for the gift.

"So I got a little something for my beautiful wife. Sue me," he said, winking at Milo and me.

As Mom opened the package she gasped, and I wondered what it could be.

"Oh, John," she whispered, her eyes flooding with emotion. "It's beautiful. I don't know what to say."

"Say you'll marry me," Dad said, kneeling down in front of my perplexed Mom, who was holding up a diamond ring, its sparkling edges catching our eye with its brilliance.

"Honey, really?" Mom laughed, as Dad took the ring from her and held it in front of her left hand.

"Well, will you?" he asked again.

"We're already married, John!" she said, still looking at the ring.

"But will you marry me again?" asked Dad, "For better or worse, richer or poorer, in sickness and in health?" Dad emphasized.

We all stared as Mom took in this information. It almost seemed unkind, pointing out the inevitable to her through a dazzling jewel. She walked over to the couch and sat down, staring off at the tree until Dad walked over and kneeled in front of her, blocking her view. "I just thought it might be nice for us to celebrate something right now," he said quietly.

"I'll marry you again, John," said Mom. "Of course I'll marry you. I said yes before and I'll say it again, over and over if I have to," she said as Dad pulled her close and they stayed locked together in an embrace, their shoulders shaking in unison as they cried in each others' arms as if nothing else mattered.

೫)ଓ

Milo and I decided to give Mom and Dad some space. "Do you want to go for a drive?" he asked me.

"Sure," I said. "I need to get out of here," I said. He nodded.

We bundled up, me in my new owl pajamas, Milo in his long johns. We walked out to Dad's car, which was covered in frost. Milo started the car, letting the defroster do some of the work while I grabbed the scraper, attacking the side windows with pent-up energy and emotion.

Milo revved the engine, signalling me to hop in, and we backed out, no real destination in sight.

"Where are we going?" I asked.

"I don't know, Hope," he said. "I'm just driving."

"Nadia," I reminded him as I looked over and saw him wipe his eyes with his shirt sleeve.

I reached over to touch his arm and he looked at me, sadness and fear reflecting back.

"God, why does it have to be like this?" he yelled, hitting the steering wheel with his balled-up fist.

"Milo, please pull over," I begged, even though the street was barren. The last thing I wanted was to die in a fiery car crash on

Christmas morning.

He pulled over onto the side of the road and covered his face with his hands, suddenly sputtering and sobbing.

I sat there, staring straight ahead. I looked around the car and realized that we had no tissues to help mop up the snot and tears.

Milo eventually calmed down and his tears dried up after a minute or so as he took some deep breaths to try and control them. He breathed in through his nose and let out a long breath through his mouth. Aside from the sniffling, it was as if his episode had never happened. Yet, as I looked at him, I could register the relief at having let it out. I was envious.

"Sorry," he said, looking at me, his eyes just slightly red, not too worse for the wear. "I didn't mean to have a meltdown."

"It's okay," I said. "You're lucky," I continued.

"Lucky?" he asked. "You mean because of my good looks?" he joked.

"Yeah," I said, mocking him. "Exactly. No, I mean, I wish I could cry."

"You mean today?" he asked.

"No, ever," I said.

"What do you mean?" he asked. "I've seen you cry plenty of times," he said.

"Not about Dad," I said, shaking my head. "Not about cancer."

"Oh," said Milo. "Well, you will. And trust me, it's nothing to be envious of. I get sad a lot," he said.

"You do?" I asked my big brother.

"Yep," he said. "I cry a lot. I'm just a big baby," he said, joking again.

"No you're not," I said. "You're the normal one."

"Hope, you're normal," he said. "Just stubborn."

"Very funny, Milo," I said. "Besides, it's Nadia now. When are you ever going to remember?"

"Exactly my point," he said. "Don't you remember Mom telling us about how your umbilical cord refused to fall off when you were a baby? The doctor kept saying, 'let's give it another week,' and finally they realized it had somehow become reattached. You've always been stubborn," said Milo.

"Yeah, I guess so," I said, looking back at the house. We'd only gotten halfway to the stop sign when Milo broke down. I figured I would need a cross-country trip to let go of the tears I had been holding back all these months.

ဢ) લ

We stayed out a bit longer, watching the steam roll around the car like smoke, holding us to that spot down the street.

Milo and I talked for another twenty minutes about his girlfriend, Carla, about school, about Dr. Ellie, about Dad.

When we got back to the house, Mom was resting on the couch and Dad was brushing a glaze over the ham we would have for dinner.

"Hi guys," he said, brightening when he saw us. "Are you okay?" he asked quietly. We both nodded.

"Big news, huh? I'm getting married!" he bellowed, bringing us both in for a group hug.

I watched Milo high-five Dad, congratulating him on "pinning down a great chic." I watched the scene take place as an outsider might watch our family, with no real investment in what was being said, what was taking place. I felt removed, yet intimately involved somehow. I wished I could capture this moment and keep it forever.

I remembered Mom's camera. I grabbed it and returned,clicking a

90

few shots of Dad and Milo putting the finishing touches on the ham. I captured my mom, prone on the sofa, her hair draped over part of her face, her diamond ring shiny and new against her aging finger, the folds on her knuckles more pronounced than the first time my dad proposed.

Dad came up behind me, wiping his sticky hands on a towel, asking if we wanted to open the rest of the presents. We whisper-screamed, "Yeah!" so as not to disturb Mom.

I glanced around the tree, looking for a flat, legal-sized present, but none fit the shape.

"Looking for something in particular?" Dad asked with a grin.

"Maybe," I said.

"Try this one," he said, handing me what was obviously not my legal documents, but clearly a book.

I tore off the paper, unwrapping my very own *Walden*. Thanks, Dad!" I said, hugging him, knowing how much the book meant to him personally.

"eBay," he said with obvious pride. "Apparently it belonged to his great-great-nephew before it was carted off to an estate sale. Look," he said, grabbing the book and opening it up, "there's his signature."

"Thoreau's?" I asked, amazed.

"Well, no, I would imagine it's his great-great-nephew's, but still," Dad said, obviously pleased with himself.

"Thanks," I said, hugging him again.

Milo got an eBay version of Steinbeck's *Of Mice and Men*, although it wasn't signed, just old, yellowed, and musty-smelling.

"Speaking of missing signatures," I said, referring to the absence of any legal paperwork. Milo and I laughed at the expression on Dad's face as he shook his head, smiling at my obviously brilliant timing.

My mom missed the whole thing, snoozing away on the couch,

the knitted green blanket separating her from us in a significant way, the bling on her finger suddenly taking on less importance than the gift of laughter Milo, Dad, and I had just unwrapped together.

I obviously still had some work to do to convince my parents that I needed to become Nadia. I just knew that life would start going our way again, once I did. That Milo could stop all his cry-baby crying and I could make this whole cancer scare nothing more than a nightmare that occasionally haunted our memories.

Next Christmas our memories would be so different.

The miserable have no other medicine
But only hope.
-William Shakespeare

PART III - *Spring*

Chapter 17

When I came home from school, Grandma was in the kitchen making sauce. The good stuff. She had sautéed a pork neck and was now mixing up the ground beef, breadcrumbs, eggs, parmesan cheese, and oregano for meatballs. We were having pasta, my dad's favorite.

"Hi sweetie," she said, greeting me warmly in a hands-free embrace.

I asked what I could do to help and she pointed to the living room with her chin, as her hands were sticky with meat mixture. I looked in and saw Mom leafing through some old family albums. She had pulled out some pictures, leaving empty spaces in the pages of our family's memories. There were several of Milo and I as babies, toddlers, and kids. I noticed a few of Dad and I set aside as well.

"Whatcha up to, Mom?" I asked, realizing that she had not noticed me standing in the same room she was occupying.

It occurred to me that she was surrounded by the memories of

Milo's and my childhood, finding refuge in the past, the photographic proof of our family's existence.

Mom turned to look at me, slowly, and in a haze. I looked over at her glass, checking its contents to see if her iced tea had been replaced with liquor. "Hi honey. I'm just reorganizing a few of these pictures. I haven't looked at them in a while."

"Do you remember this camping trip?" she asked, pointing to a picture of Milo and me, ages seven and three, respectively, standing next to a life-size Yogi Bear sign at Yellowstone National Park.

"Isn't that the trip when you started screaming for us to evacuate the tent in the middle of the night because you thought an airplane was crashing?"

She chuckled, "Yeah. It sounded so close out there in the middle of the forest."

She looked at me, then, and I noticed the tears glinting in her eyes. I surveyed the coffee table and took note of the small pile of used tissues.

"Do you want to know what I was thinking on that trip?" she asked, grabbing another tissue. "I remember thinking that we were the luckiest family in the world, surrounded by the canopy of trees, with the stars beaming down on us. I could see your little face looking up at me. You were scared to death. I had scared you to death, and your dad picked you up, hugged you tight, and we all huddled up together in the tent to try and fall back asleep."

She blotted at her eyes with the tissue, grabbed my hand, and said, "We were so damn lucky."

All through my dad's favorite dinner I chewed, and smiled, and laughed as Grandma spilled little globs of sauce on her shirt, as always. I ate just as I always did, asking for a second helping of penne to go along with my third helping of meatballs.

I ate and ate, but tasted only the bitter, salty tears my mom had shed.

ℰℭ

March 4

Dearest Nadia,

Spring is in the air, can't you smell it? I guess you wouldn't know it by its smell since you spent your childhood on the West Coast, but I recognize spring by its muskiness. A smell born of snow melting into the dry earth, creating a moist scent that verges on mildew. I know we have a couple of weeks yet before the good smells pop up – the tulips and daffodils and grape hyacinths (my favorite sign of spring, by the way), but this smell, this beginning of new life is what awakens my senses from their hibernation after a long winter breathing stale, recycled air. Don't you just love it?

Some people might wish for spring all year long, but not me. I know for a fact that I could never appreciate this wonderful time of year if I experienced it every day. It is the doldrums of winter that make spring so wonderous.

I love you, Dad

Maybe Dad was right, I thought. Maybe spring was a time of year worth honoring. I decided to find out.

I grabbed Mom's camera, which I seemed to be using more and more lately, sought out a fleece jacket, and headed outside.

Our house showed signs of being a rental most now. There were little green shoots popping up out of the ground. Tulips, it appeared, and daffodils. They looked to be in no certain order, planted willy-nilly

97

around the border of the house. There even seemed to be a patch of flowers growing up in a circular formation smack-dab in the middle of the front yard. It was bizarre. Normally such a circle would surround a tree or other structure, but nothing existed here. The big oak tree out back was left unadorned, I learned later, so this circular patch seemed to serve no purpose.

I took a picture of it, as it fit nicely with my theme of photographing the everyday odd. Then I remembered the features of my mom's camera. I clicked a few buttons, changing the color setting to sepia, then shot a few more. I zoomed in on the bud of a tulip and clicked the button.

I made my way around back and found it littered with small branches, broken from a long winter of frost, snow, ice, and gusty winds.

I walked around, hunched over, gathering up a pile of these small sticks and twigs, placing them in a tidy bundle at the base of the oak. I glanced over at the neighbor's house and noticed just a hint of purple peeking out at me from the mulch they had heaped on the previous fall.

I headed over and confirmed that Dad's favorite sign of spring was already in bloom. I crouched down and ran my fingers over the tiny purple flowers, aptly named for their perfectly round bluish-purple blossoms. I swung Mom's camera around, reset the color to vibrant and snapped a few pictures of the grape hyacinths.

I walked back to the oak tree and gathered up the bundle of sticks I had collected, carrying them around to the front yard. I dropped them in the middle of the circle of flowers, yet to bloom, and began poking the sticks into the hard earth until there were twenty or so jutting out of the ground. When I was finished, it resembled the candles of a birthday cake, evenly spaced within the boundary of flowers.

I took a few pictures of my creation and considered that soon the flowers would grow and tower over the sticks. As I replaced the lens on the camera and treaded back to the house, I thought of a name for my work of art: Everything Has a Season.

It might not have been Dr. Ellie's idea of journaling, but I did feel as if my artistic behavior was an appropriate response to my emotions.

Little did I know how appropriate my art would prove to be.

Chapter 18

Mom and Dad decided to renew their vows on the first official day of spring: March 20th, which happened to be a Tuesday. Not a particularly festive day of the week, but the symbolism of renewal was more important to them than convenience, apparently.

Mom asked me to serve as her bridesmaid, and Dad asked Milo to be his groomsman.

"Aren't you taking this a little far?" I asked Dad one afternoon, after I heard him on the phone bickering with Sunny's Florist about the price of roses.

"Haven't you heard, Nadia? Extreme Weddings. It's the newest rage," he joked.

"Exactly my point," I said. "W-E-D-D-I-N-G," I spelled out. "You've been married for 18 years. Why the fuss?" But, to tell you the truth, I was a little bit excited about the impending nuptials, even if they would be déjà vu for my parents. It's unfair that most kids don't get the opportunity to be part of their parents' wedding. And those who are, well, they're definitely not the norm, at least not in Ohio.

Mom and Dad keep their wedding album displayed with the other photo albums on the bookshelf, and I sneak a peek at it from time to time. In it, I am able to get a hint of what Dad's parents might have been like, based on their smiles and Grandma's oversized navy floral dress. She had short reddish hair, similar to the color of mine. It definitely wasn't as wavy, but it had some volume. Fortunately, I didn't inherit her thick ankles.

Grandpa looked really tall next to Dad, which must have put him around six feet two or three inches. He was super thin and nearly bald. Handsome, in a differerent way than Dad. More like a John Wayne type. Masculine, where Dad looked the part of an academic.

Mom was stunning. Her white gown was simple, yet elegant. The bodice was beaded and off-the-shoulder, nicely offsetting its straight, silky skirt. She didn't wear a veil, but did have a beaded headband, which matched her dress. Her heels must have been significant, because she was nearly as tall as Dad in the photos, where normally she comes up to his nose.

Dad wore a dark grey suit. "Not black," he told me. "Most grooms wear black. I wanted to stand out a bit." His smile, the biggest of anyone's in the album did, in fact, make him stand out. He looked radiant, a description usually reserved for the bride.

I guess it made sense, all the fuss. Weddings were clearly a special day, and renewing your vows, especially when one involves sickness and health, is a major commitment. Not for the weak of heart.

Dad just smiled and ignored my complaining about all the fuss, choosing instead to redial the phone to get a quote from another florist.

Chapter 19

I woke up on the first day of spring with a sinking feeling in the pit of my stomach. *Butterflies?* I wondered, thinking about the lavender dress Mom had picked out for me to wear to the ceremony this evening. I hadn't wanted purple, but Mom managed to convice me that it contrasted nicely with the reddish tones in my hair.

All I could think about this morning were the dirty lavender walls in mine and Milo's bedrooms. In fact, as I lay there, I scanned the room noticing how much more pleasant the color was in the early morning light. Deeper, less pastel than in daylight's sharp focus.

Suddenly I couldn't bear the thought of that ugly lavender dress. *What could I do to make it less hideous?* I wondered.

And then I remembered the jeans Mom had bought me last weekend, the same day as the dress. I hadn't worn them yet, so the denim was still steeped in all of that indigo dye. *Maybe some of it will come out in the wash and darken the dress a little.* It was worth a try.

I grabbed the dress, which was hanging in my closet, still shrouded in its plastic bag, along with the jeans. I cut the tags off of both and headed to the garage, to the wash basin to soak the dress and jeans together for a bit. I knew the dress would need a few hours to dry, since it couldn't go in the dryer.

I turned on the faucet, allowing the water to run warm, plugged the drain and closed my eyes, plunging the lavender dress into the tub. I peeked, squinting through one eye, then both upon seeing that all was well. I added the jeans and grabbed a yardstick from the pile of tools to stir them together. I felt like a witch over a cauldron, stirring my strange brew. *All I need is eye of newt,* I chuckled to myself.

Deciding that my concoction needed a good soaking, I went inside to grab breakfast and catch an episode of iCarly that I had recorded yesterday. Sam and Carly were timing each other slugging a huge jug of tomato juice while Freddie captured it all on film. Gross.

Milo came downstairs, yawning and stretching in front of the TV.

"Really?" I asked. "Of all the places to stand down here, you choose right in front of the TV?"

"How else am I going to show off these muscles?" he joked, making a fist and pumping his arms.

"Right," I said.

"Are you ready for the big event?" he asked.

"I guess. Are you?"

"I'm the groomsman. My job is to make sure the groom shows up. I think I'm up for the challenge," he said with a grin.

"Let's hope Mom doesn't take one look at the groom and run off," I said, wondering if I might choose that option, given the circumstance.

"Let's hope Mom doesn't take one look at you in your bridesmaid dress and run off," he joked.

That reminded me. "Gotta go get ready for school," I said, heading to the garage to check on my dress, hoping for a nice deep purple.

I knew something was wrong as soon as I approached the sink. Big bubbles of lavender fabric were floating on the surface, apparently having escaped from underneath the weight of the jeans. I stirred the mixture and watched as the remainder of my dress floated to the surface, tie-dyed in the worst sense of the word. Large splotches of indigo covered the once-fair dress, giving it a mottled appearance. Neither color was pretty.

Mom was going to kill me.

I drained the sink and removed my jeans, squeezing the water out of them and setting them on the side of the tub. I turned on the faucet, and let the cool water run over the dress, hoping to rinse out the dark patches. Some of the color did run down the drain, but the effect was still permanent: I had ruined the dress.

I took it upstairs and hung it up in my closet, covering it with the plastic wrap, thinking I could feign innocence. "I can't imagine what could have happened. We must have had a break-in!"

Yes, someone must have broken into our rental home for the sole purpose of dyeing a bridesmaid dress. I was toast. I got ready for school and went downstairs.

"Good morning, Hope, er Nadia," said Mom, coffee in hand, rushing around the kitchen in her pajamas.

"Are you staying home today?" I asked.

"Yes, I took the day off so I could clean before our company arrives. Could you do me a favor and bring your dress downstairs so I can iron it?"

Oh boy.

"Uh, Mom, I think we need to talk," I said.

She stopped in her tracks. Apparently this was a phrase that made parents do that sort of thing. "What?" she asked, in a clipped tone as if she were prepared for the worst possible news. The news I was about to deliver.

"There's something wrong with my dress," I said.

"What do you mean?" she asked. "Did it rip? I can fix it, just bring it downstairs."

"Um, no, it's not ripped, it's more, uh, well, I kind of…"

"Spit it out, Hope! What's wrong with your dress?" she accused, rightfully.

"Nadia," I said.

"Excuse me?" she asked, daring me to repeat myself.

I let it slide, instead opting to tell her the ugly truth, "I dyed it."

"You dyed it," she said, a statement, not a question.

"Well, I tried to dye it. See, I was lying in bed looking around the room and I noticed…"

"You DYED IT?" she yelled.

"You didn't let me finish," I said. "I TRIED to dye it, but…"

"HOPE ELIZABETH WALLACE!" she yelled, "What did you do to your dress?"

I sighed. Clearly she wasn't interested in hearing my story, or calling me by the proper name. I turned around and walked out of the room, heading to my room to claim my prize so I could show her exactly what I had done, but she was having none of it.

"DON''T YOU WALK AWAY FROM ME!" she yelled. "I AM SO ANGRY RIGHT NOW I COULD JUST, I COULD JUST!"

"What, Mom, you could just what?" I asked as calmly as I could.

"I COULD JUST…" She slapped me. Hard. Right across my cheek.

I was stunned. I watched her face melt from a mask of rage to a pleading look of sorrow. Ruining my dress had been an act of betrayal on this, the day of her renewal of vows. But it was not her husband betraying her, it was her thirteen year-old daughter, caught in an act of defiance so dastardly it deserved a physical response.

Never before had my mother hit me. Never had I felt the sting of rage on any part of my body. When other parents were swatting their kids' bottoms, my mom was calmly taking away privileges. I was the product of progressive parenting, up until now. But this slap? It represented the undoing of all of that. This was war. Okay, maybe I had dipped my toe into enemy territory, but Mom's response, her atomic bomb, was completely out of line.

I had dyed a dress, for heaven's sake, not dressed up to avoid the reality of dying.

And that's when I realized that Mom wasn't mad about the dress. Not really. She was angry about my dad. Mad that things would never go her way again. Apparently she hadn't gotten the memo that there was no 'I' in 'Team.'

Dr. Ellie was so wrong.

Chapter 20

The drama of the morning carried into my day. I missed the bus and had to ask Mom for a ride to school. Trust me, asking Mom for a favor was the last thing I wanted to do. It was a silent drive with no words exchanged. It made me so uncomfortable that I reached into the deepest recesses of my backpack looking for a piece of gum. I found three pieces of cinnamon Trident and stuck them all in my mouth, counting on the chomping to add some ambiance to the trip.

She dropped me off at school without a word.

"Bye," I said sweetly, as I climbed out of the car.

"Goodbye," she said, still angry.

Whatever, I thought, as I headed up the steps. *Get over it.* The first bell had already rung, so I didn't have time to stop at my locker. I dropped my backpack off outside the door of the classroom and went in, unprepared, without a pencil or paper.

"Pop quiz," said Ms. Singleton in her sing-song voice. "I hope

109

you've been studying the parts of speech like I told you," she said.

The whole class groaned. At least I wasn't the only one.

At lunch, I bumped into a sixth grader, causing her to dump her tray all over the floor.

"Hope," called Mr. Glasky, the Assistant Principal, "grab a mop and clean it up," he said, unsympathetic to the fact that it was the pip-squeak sixth grader's fault for stopping right in front of me.

"But Mr. Glasky," I said.

"Now, Hope," he said, the second adult to cut me off in a period of hours, "do I need to ask twice?"

He didn't.

On the bus ride home I zoned out, exhausted. As we made the turn into our neighborhood and neared the rental house I saw Grandma's and Aunt Susan's cars parked in the driveway.

Great, I thought, *let the party begin*.

And it had, I saw, as I opened the front door. The living room had been completely reconfigured, with the couches gone, replaced by two rows of white folding chairs, each tied with a single red rose. White chiffon was draped along the row, attaching the chairs together in one long chain. There was a red runner on the floor in between the two rows of chairs. Honestly, it looked beautiful.

Grandma met me in the kitchen with a hug. "Hope, honey, how was your day?" she asked, squeezing a bit of spirit back into me.

"It was fine," I said, too exhausted from my day to break the news to my grandmother about Nadia. "Looks like you've been busy. The living room looks great."

"Your mother and your aunt did all that," she said. "In fact, I think your mother had most of it finished before Susan arrived. Either she's really excited or she poured an extra cup of coffee this morning," said Grandma.

110

Good, she didn't know.

"Oh, by the way, honey," she said, "here's your dress. I just finished ironing it. It's really lovely."

I rolled my eyes, remembering the particularly hideous mottled mess of lavender and indigo, and walked back to the kitchen to retrieve it. To my amazement, it wasn't anything like I remembered. It was black as night and beautiful.

I knocked on Mom's door and, upon receiving no reply, entered. She was attempting to zip up the back of her dress, a knee-length black, sequined dress that looked nothing like I had imagined the bride-to-be wearing on her renewal of vows day.

"Wow, you look amazing," I said, startling her.

"Thanks," she said with a shy smile, and I realized in that moment that my mom was really beautiful. She didn't have perfect hair, or perfect teeth, or perfectly toned legs, but she was so pretty standing there in her black dress, sparking my memory.

"Thanks for the dress," I said, holding it out in front of me.

"You tried to tell me that the other one was too babyish, but I didn't listen. I'm so sorry, honey. I'm sorry for the dress, I'm sorry that I hurt you, and I'm sorry for being so crazy. You deserve better," she said, sniffing.

"Hey, don't cry," I said, going to her. "You'll mess up your mascara. Dad doesn't really go for goth," I said and we both laughed. "I'm sorry too," I said. "I made it about me. It's not. It's about you and Dad, or at least I think it's about you and Dad. Honestly, I don't really understand the point of all this," I said.

She laughed again, a good sign, then sighed.

"I'm sure it seems really stupid, but honey, when you've loved someone for as long as your dad and I have loved each other, you just go a little nuts when something threatens it. I think that's what we're doing. Going a little nuts. But we've got cake, and, hey, I hired Jack to come do our hair and make-up. What do you think? Maybe a little nuts is exactly what we need right now."

And you know what? I couldn't have agreed more. It turned out that the ceremony was not only completely nuts, but really amazing too. Mom recreated the vows she spoke eighteen years ago, at their "real" wedding whereas Dad wrote something entirely new, just for the occasion.

"Anna," he said, looking into her eyes, which I could see from my vantage point directly beside her. In fact, Milo and Dad stood next to each other too, the four of us creating a rectangle with our bodies serving as the four corners.

"I know it sounds cliché to say I love you more now than I did all those years ago, but it's true. Back then I loved you because I thought you were perfect. But now," he said, shaking his head and grinning slightly, "I love you despite the evidence that you're far from it." Mom smiled.

Dad continued, "I love your wrinkles and your stubborness, your quick-temper and your bad morning breath. I even love you despite your insistence that Hemingway was a drunk," he said, teasing her as she chuckled.

"But mostly," he went on, taking a deep breath and lowering his voice to a near-whisper, "I love you because you love me. A man consumed by fear. A father who can do so little for his children right now. A child in so many ways. You love me and show me every day that your kind of love is boundless."

They kissed, we all hugged, and my family felt whole for the first time in months. I closed my eyes and wished it could last forever.

Chapter 21

I blame Mr. Fallon. For the second time in a month, he pulled me aside after class for a pow-wow.

"Have you gotten to know Grace Powers?" he asked.

"Uh, you mean the girl who sits up front with her posse?" I asked.

He didn't take the bait. "I had Grace's older sister a couple of years ago. Nice family. Good girls. You might consider it," he suggested in a way that made me feel like I owed him something, even though he really hadn't done anything but notice me for the reality of my situation. This certainly did not put him at the top of my list of favorite people.

But I made the mistake of running into Grace in the hall and, in a momentary lapse of judgement, gave her enough of a smile that she waved. This created a stir in her posse, who also waved. I had been noticed by people my own age for the first time since we moved to Ohio. It was weird.

That night Grace called me.

"Hope, er Nadia, phone!" Mom yelled up the stairs. Ever since Mom and Dad's renewal of vows ceremony, we had been especially polite with each other. Frankly, it felt a little odd.

"Who is it?" I asked with the perplexity of a girl who hadn't received a phone call in weeks.

"Someone named Grace. She sounds nice!" Mom yelled, with an eagerness in her voice like I was a little lost puppy she was trying to place with a nice family.

I picked up the phone with a "Hello?"

"Hi Hope, it's Grace from homeroom. How are you?" she asked, with the hint of pity I had become accustomed to hearing from everyone.

"I'm fine," I said. *Short and sweet*, I thought to myself. *Keep it short and sweet.*

"My mom, I mean, I wondered if you wanted to come over Friday night for a sleepover," she asked, though her slip-up clued me in to the real motive behind this surprise phone call.

"This Friday?" I asked, as if I had a full schedule to consider.

"Yeah. Casey, Mara, and I are going to hang out and watch some scary movies. Want to come?"

I looked up to see my mom standing in my doorway shaking her head 'yes' vigorously. She must have thrown me off because I agreed.

"Six o'clock," she said. "We'll order a pizza when everyone gets here."

"OK," I agreed. "Oh, by the way, you're in my science and English classes too," I mentioned before hanging up the phone, but I think she was already gone.

℘ℭ

I guess I can admit that I was a little excited about the sleepover. I missed my BFF Abby like crazy every day, and hadn't considered that there might be others who would be willing to get to know me and my crazy family.

After school, I quickly wrapped up a couple of assignments that I had left over from math and Spanish. I figured it would be best to get them out of the way so I could enjoy myself with the girls tonight.

As Dad drove me to the sleepover, I navigated with the directions Grace had written down at school that day. She already knew where I lived but I didn't ask how, assuming that everyone in the school knew about our situation and had driven by the house with the circus freaks residing inside.

"Look," I imagined them saying as they pointed. "It's Hope's house, where perfectly healthy people get sick! Drive away, drive away, before cancer's gravitational pull sucks you in!"

"Is this it?" Dad asked, as we pulled into the driveway of a cape-cod style brick home, with dormer-style windows upstairs. I imagined Grace and her sister sharing the one large room upstairs, with its angled walls, nooks, and crannies. A perfect bedroom for two perfect sisters.

"Are you okay?" Dad asked, as I continued to sit in the front seat staring down at my orange Converse shoes, the ones I had inked up with little peace signs on a particularly upbeat day.

"Yeah," I said softly. "I'm fine."

"Do you want me to walk you up?" he asked.

"No," I said, more sharply than intended. "I'm okay, really," I assured him (and myself), as I got out of the car and reached into the backseat for my duffel bag and sleeping bag. Pink with purple peace signs. Ugh.

Her mom opened the door. At least I assume it was her mom. She

115

looked just like Grace, only taller and more beautiful. She was in jeans and a t-shirt, but was so pretty that the casual outfit looked entirely glamorous. "You must be Hope," she said, smiling and ushering me inside while waving to my dad, who was backing out of the driveway. "I'm so glad you could come. Please call me Pam," she said, wearing what I now realized was her signature smile. "Grace has told me all about you," she said, then, realizing the implications, bumbled around a little. "I mean, Grace has told me that she was excited to get to know you better."

Really? This was news to me.

Grace and the rest of the posse came downstairs and rescued me from the clutches of Perfect Pam.

"Moms," Grace said, rolling her eyes, as she directed me upstairs to the room I had envisioned, right down to the nooks and crannies. My mind's eye had imagined it perfectly, all except for the Chia Pet.

There, in one of the windows was a terra-cotta dog growing green buds. I had seen the commercials, but never a real-and-true Chia. I was drawn to it, something about the care that had been put into the planting of seeds and watering of this strange man-made plant. It made me think of my mom and the reality of teaching about trees versus living among them. All of a sudden I was terribly sad.

"What do you guys want to watch tonight?" Grace asked, interrupting my train of thought, "I ordered a few movies from Netflix."

I didn't mean to say it. It just popped out, and I regretted it immediately. "Scary movies, right? Did you get the one about the father of two dying of cancer?"

It was just like that old saying, "She stopped them in their tracks." The girls froze, like statues, staring at me with their mouths wide open.

Grace placed the DVD's on her bed and excused herself. The

116

posse followed, and I was left alone in the bedroom of my dreams.

I heard a door slam then, "Why did you make me invite her?" Grace yelled at Perfect Pam. "She's trying to ruin everything! She's creepy and weird – did you see her outfit?"

I glanced down at my bright purple jeans and could see nothing weird – or creepy – about pairing them with a red and yellow sunset t-shirt, a favorite that Abby had picked out for me in a Venice Beach surf shop last summer. Abby would have been rolling on the floor laughing if she were here right now.

"Honey, you need to think about her situation," Perfect Pam cooed in muffled tones. "She's new to town and is surely lonely. I feel just terrible about her family's situation. Just try to imagine, sweetheart."

I thought it interesting that she was trying to reason with a girl who spent the entire homeroom period primping and putting on makeup behind the book blockade she set up at her desk.

"I don't care about her family!" Grace hollered, surely loudly enough that she must have known I heard. And I can't really blame her on this point. No one in her right mind would want to start caring about my family right now. There was a guaranteed let-down at the end.

"She's sarcastic and weird and I don't want her here! She doesn't fit in!" Grace punctuated.

And she was right, I didn't fit in. Not in this Barbie Dreamhouse. Grace's life was happy and easy, drama-free. She couldn't relate to the dark thoughts I couldn't stop from constantly creeping into my mind. She thinks *Halloween* is scary, but in horror movies the slashing is inevitable. In real life, when evil pops up, the terror is completely unexpected.

I looked around the room one last time before making my escape.

117

I knew I would never see it again, but wanted to capture a picture of it in my mind, the two twin beds coming out from under the large angled spaces where the windows jutted out, the perfectly soothing blue-green color that either Grace or her sister had picked out from the thousands of samples at the paint store, the map of the world with big red dots on London and Alaska, places I dreamed of seeing, but had yet to go.

It made no sense, Grace with this perfect room, living in a perfect home with Perfect Pam, and her perfect dad (whom I didn't get to meet, but assumed his perfection nonetheless).

Grace was a neanderthal, deserving of a cave to dwell in, with charcoal stick-figures of deer, and fires in constant need of stoking. Grace did not deserve this room, with the perfect Chia Dog.

So, I took it. I released the hound from its imprisonment within the walls of Grace's room, grabbed my stuff, and took the steps two-at-a-time.

I passed the girls, standing in the kitchen with Perfect Pam, waved and smiled, leaving them with an invitation of my own, "Just so you know, my name is actually Nadia, but you don't need to bother learning it. Oh, and I just remembered that I have to go clean my dad's bedpan. Anyone want to come help?"

I burst out into the cool dusk, not waiting for an answer.

Chapter 22

I didn't feel like talking to Dr. Ellie today, but I had no choice. Mom had freaked out after I walked home from the slumber party. She couldn't understand what had happened, even when I tried to explain that Grace was evil.

"Do we need to set up an emergency session with Dr. Ellie?" she asked.

"No mom, it's fine, really. She was never going to be my best friend."

She didn't buy it and called Dr. Ellie at home. Hence my appointment today.

"Couldn't we just grab some ice cream or something?" I asked her as we circled the block, looking for a parking spot.

"Nadia, I don't have time for this," she sighed, craning her neck around to attempt a parallel-parking job in between two cars parked right up against the painted lines marking the boundary between the spots.

"Sor-ry," I said sarcastically, yet secretly pleased that she had remembered not to call me Hope.

She sighed again and tore out of the unmanageable tight space, circling the block once more before deciding to drop me off out front.

"There's not a spot in sight. I'm going to run to the grocery instead. I'll pick you up after your session. I should be back, but wait for me right here if I'm running a little late," she warned me as she pealed away.

"As if you would care if I walked home," I muttered as I climbed the steps to Dr. Ellie's office.

"Hello Nadia," Dr. Ellie greeted me, along with her usual warm smile.

"Hi," I said, the corners of my mouth turned down to match the mood I was in.

We sat. I picked her chair this time, the white, slipcovered chair with the flowered pillow, just to see what she would do. She took the rocker. I realized then that Dr. Ellie always waited to sit down until after I had picked my seat. I hadn't sat in "her" chair after all. She owned them all, and was somehow placing some psychological meaning in my choice of seats.

I didn't like it.

"I changed my mind," I said, standing up. "Can we switch?"

"Seats?" she asked, standing. "Of course, Nadia, wherever you are most comfortable is fine with me," she said, annoying me further with her compliance.

"What if I said I wanted to sit on the floor?" I asked.

"Do you want to sit on the floor?" she asked, answering my question with a question.

"Maybe," I said. "But what if I wanted you to sit on the floor too?"

"Then let's sit on the floor," she said, grabbing a large pillow hidden from view on the other side of the couch. *This woman is good*, I thought.

"Nah," I said. "I'm just going to lay down on the couch."

"Great," she said. "The couch it is." She sat back down in the rocking chair, scooting it toward me so she could see my face.

"Tell me about your journaling, Nadia," she said, "What have you learned about yourself recently?"

"Well, that I'm no good at journaling, for one," I said.

"No good?" she asked.

"I haven't been doing it," I admitted.

"I see," she said, writing something in her own notepad. "Well, it does take practice and daily discipline, much like learning to type, which, by the way, I didn't do until I was forty-two," she said, smiling. "I truly believe you will come to enjoy journaling a great deal, once you get into the habit," she said.

"I don't see why I can't just talk to you about stuff," I said. "It's easier."

"You can," she said, "but journaling involves more risk. And more reward. In writing your thoughts, you become accountable to no one but yourself. This form of free expression allows you to share with yourself bits and pieces that I wouldn't expect you to feel comfortable sharing with anyone – even your therapist. When you're mad? Write it down. And write why. Is it your mom? Your dad? A friend? It's your journal, Nadia, and nobody but you will ever read it. It's all right to share your thoughts with the one person who knows and understands these feelings without fear of judgement or retribution: you."

"Well, I'll try," I said, "but I make no guarantees."

"And no guarantees need be made. You aren't doing this for me,

Nadia. I'm not grading you, or assessing you on your journaling. Think of it as giving yourself a pass. Whatever you write down on those pages can live there and there alone. You may find that once the words appear on the page you feel a freedom within, as if they have escaped from a cage and fluttered onto the page."

"Ok, I'll give it another shot," I said. "For me."

"Good, Nadia, I'm glad you are willing to give yourself a chance. Now, would you like to discuss what happened last night and your mother's response to it?" she asked.

"Do we have to?" I asked.

"It is entirely up to you," she said, smiling at me.

"I think I would rather forget about it and move on," I told her earnestly. "Maybe write about it in my journal," I added as an afterthought.

"Excellent," said Dr. Ellie. "Sometimes when we express ourselves through writing we find the courage and strength to truly move on."

I guess, I thought to myself, wondering if moving on was really an option. Or that I cared.

Chapter 23

It started out like a normal Thursday. I had procrastinated studying for my math quiz, so in between bites of English muffin I scrambled to work out the algebra problems on the prep sheet Mrs. Maloney had passed out. Dad would normally offer to quiz me, but I glanced over and noticed him observing his coffee. It certainly looked all right to me, piping hot, with a healthy dose of creamer. He lifted the mug to his lips and sipped the world's smallest sip. He looked up and I saw the concern on his face.

"You okay, Dad?" I asked, mentally struggling to come up with the factor of $(x -15) + 7 = 6$.

"Um, sure, honey. I'm fine. I just need to find your mom," he said not at all convincingly before abandoning his coffee and leaving me alone with my math.

"Good luck on your quiz today, Hopie," he called from the hall.

"Hopie?"

Milo, who must have passed Dad in the hall, bustled into the kitchen, grabbed a waffle from the freezer, and popped it into the toaster.

"Something's wrong," I said.

"I can help you if you don't understand," he said scooting a chair next to me, glancing at the math notes I had taken the previous day.

"Not with math, Milo, with Dad," I said, irritated. It seemed I was the only one who picked up on anything going on around here.

"Besides cancer?" he said, trying to be funny, but as soon as he said it I could sense the regret in his face.

"I mean, of course there's something wrong, Hope. Dad is sick. And he's sick and tired of being sick and tired."

"Cut the lecture, Milo," I seethed. "There's something else wrong. Dad is acting funny this morning, and it doesn't have anything to do with being sick and tired."

I was keenly aware of Milo's eyes on mine. We both knew how perceptive I was, and the kitchen grew quiet as we gathered in this new bit of information, holding it against our chests, a tightening that intensified until the waffle popping out of the toaster broke the spell and Milo got up to finish preparing his breakfast.

Figuring factors seemed a worthless exercise, so Milo and I ate our breakfasts in silence. Mom emerged then, grabbed a granola bar and apple, then searched for the one to-go coffee mug we owned. She located it behind the regular mugs and poured a cup of steaming coffee, black and hot. She screwed the lid on tightly and walked to the table to grab Dad's coffee, now lukewarm at best, pouring it down the drain. She turned to us and announced, almost defensively, that Dad was fine, but she was taking him to the hospital.

She shrugged off Milo's inquiry as to what was going on and said, "He's feeling a little under the weather."

In typical fashion, she left us reeling with anxiety, expecting that we simply go to school, ace our math quizzes, make nice with our friends, and ignore what we both agreed was not a good sign.

ഇൻ

It was a bad sign, indeed. I learned a new word today: metastasize. And I would come to learn the repercussions of its meaning in less than a month's time.

Dad noticed, almost overnight, a tightening in his throat, and knew something wasn't right. Apparently cancer has a few tricks up its sleeves. We had arrived at Stage IV.

We all spent the afternoon with Dad at the hospital. I brought a deck of cards and we half-heartedly played Joker Poker. Mom was distracted, glancing out into the hallway every minute or so, as if she were attempting to catch sight of someone she knew. At one point Dad confirmed my suspicion, saying, "Anna, he said he would stop by tonight. It's not even four-thirty." Mom said nothing, but picked up a queen, inserting it into the spot across from an ace.

"Mom!" I exclaimed. "That was dumb. You just gave yourself eleven points!" She looked up at me with eyes that nearly made me cry. Sad eyes, which almost allowed you to see right down to her broken heart, "If I thought I could win I would hold out for an ace, but at this point I just want to get it over with."

Her comment made me realize that the game had changed again. It was no longer Dad vs. Cancer. It was Cancer vs. Dad.

My dad looked at her and softly said, "Anna, why don't you go grab a coffee. I want to talk to Milo and Hope."

Mom shook her head in agreement and rifled through her purse, coming up with a couple of dollars. She crossed the small room, stopped at the door and looked back as if she were going to ask if we would like anything, but changed her mind and exited without a word.

Neither Milo nor I wanted to ask. We knew. We didn't know the details at that point, but we knew. And Dad knew we knew. It was then that I learned the new word.

"It's not good, guys," Dad said. "The tumors in my lungs have metastasized to my throat. It's very aggressive and fast-growing. At this point Dr. Phillips doesn't think it will respond to chemo. He's conferencing with a specialist in Texas about the possibility of radiation to shrink it, and we'll know later tonight what they decide."

Milo asked Dad if it hurt and Dad said it was uncomfortable, made it difficult to swallow, but that he was not in any more pain than before.

I couldn't help it. I swallowed. I learned last year about autonomic responses, like breathing and blinking, that your brain takes care of for you. You don't think about doing these things, but your brain does. Swallowing too. It was a strange feeling, to consider this routine bodily function. I am only aware of my throat when it hurts, like the two times I have had strep throat and felt the swelling take over, changing the way my voice sounded. I imagined how Dad must feel, knowing there was a tumor in there. Could he feel it? Was swallowing now something he would have to prepare for each and every time? Both reasonable questions that my dad, determined to be honest with us no matter what, would have answered.

But the only question I could come up with, however, in that moment where ugly truths were revealed was, "Who wants a Coke?" followed by my immediate departure in search of the nearest vending machine.

Chapter 24

I was numb. And not numb like the way I felt that morning I spent in the snow a few months' earlier. That numbness was specific to my nose, fingers, and toes. This encircled me fully, making it difficult to breathe. My mind, usually sharp and responsive, was mush.

Tonight in the hospital felt like the true beginning of my dad's death sentence. His last meal was beef stroganoff with a perfect little mound of mashed potatoes. And, as you might expect, lime Jell-O. He ate less than he left behind for the nurse to haul away.

We played a few more hands of cards, but silently. I couldn't help stealing quick glances at my dad, catching him eyeing me with that horrible look of pity I had come to know so well.

I looked away, heart racing. *This was it. Had to be it. Dad had succumbed not only to cancer, but to the belief that he was leaving us.*

As I hugged him when we were leaving, he whispered in my ear, "Check your pillow, Nadia."

I jerked my head up to look at him, his eyes changed, no longer pitying, but gleaming with excitement. *Was it true?*

The world had just shifted on its axis, and I began trembling in pace with the earthquake of emotions that passed through my body.

⁗⁗

I took the stairs two at a time, bounding with an energy and excitement that confused even me.

My pillow was exactly as I had left it, but as I dug my hand underneath, I pulled out a manila envelope. My manila envelope. My heart pounded.

I brought it to my lips, kissing it for luck. As I slowly unwound the red string holding it together, I thought about my dad's timing. *Why now?* I wondered.

As I slid out the three-page document, a handwritten note fluttered onto my bed.

April 1

Dearest Nadia,

You are possibly the most persistent person I know! I mean this as a compliment, of course, and feel confident that you will put this quality to use for the greater good as you grow older and wiser.

As for me, I am not sure how much older (or wiser, for that matter) I am destined to grow. For that reason, I have made a difficult decision. I have decided to give you the gift of my signature. I know you, honey. Have known you ever since the moment when I looked into your big brown eyes for the first time thirteen and a half years ago. I understand what you need now, and I'm willing to let go in order for you to get it. I understand that you need to become Nadia, and I can respect that. I can give you that. I just need for you to know that, to me, you will always be Hope.

I love you, Dad

Wiping away tears, I paged through the document, taking the time to look at the bottom of each page, where I had stuck an arrow-shaped red post-it to mark the signature lines. Each was filled in with the shape and curve of my dad's signature: a big looping 'J', followed by illegible squiggles. Even the 'W' in Wallace was indistinguishable as part of the whole.

Dad's sloppy handwriting aside, I was holding a legal document with my dad's signature allowing me the right to appear in court, in front of Judge Mann, to make Nadia official.

In asking him to sign these forms, I wondered if I had wounded my dad in a critical sort of way. In order for me to have my desire, did he have to give up a piece of himself? A piece he was in no shape to give? Or perhaps it was his last-ditch effort to save himself; to see this in the same way I did, as an opportunity.

It made me dizzy with possibility and, for the first time since we moved to Ohio, I felt hopeful.

Chapter 25

I had to ride my bike to Dr. Ellie's this afternoon, with Dad in the hospital and Mom staying with him. Although Milo technically has his license, I've never counted on him to get me from place-to-place. He's always busy with soccer or track after school. Besides, I've always loved riding my bike, or at least I used to, before I moved to Youngstown and the landscape became so flat and uninspired.

My favorite place to ride out in California was this trail just south of the Klamath Mountains, where there were signs posted warning of mountain lions. Past the desert scrub, I occasionally saw lizards sunning themselves on the pebbly trail, often camouflaged so well that the sudden movement, as they escaped from being crushed by a bicycle tire, could be construed as a figment of one's imagination. I realized how much I missed those lizards, and their ability to blend seamlessly and adapt quickly.

I pulled up to Dr. Ellie's office and dismounted my bike, realizing

I had forgotten my lock. I pulled off my helmet and tucked it under my armpit, where it competed with my backpack for space. I thought about ditching my appointment, but was excited to show Dr. Ellie the signed forms I had been carrying with me for the past five days. I took the stairs to her second floor office two at a time.

As I opened the outer door to her office, I frightened a woman who was attending to her tissue and purse, ignoring the mysterious pull of the door until she nearly fell over as it opened more abruptly than she expected. This woman was a mess. Mascara stains ran down the corners of her puffy eyes and she was heaving breath in and out nearly hysterically.

I wondered why Dr. Ellie didn't stop her from going. As a therapist, wasn't her job to make people feel better, not worse? I stepped out of the way as I held the door for this sobbing mess who might have been attractive in any other circumstance. She slunk past me, choking on the air as she headed for the stairs. I wanted to stop and shake her. Didn't she know what she looked like? Why was she such a mess? I became aware of my helmet's straps digging into my side, and shook the sight of the woman out of my mind. I took a deep breath and headed into the confines of Dr. Ellie's office.

"Hello Nadia," said Dr. Ellie, a bit more reserved than usual.

"Hi!" I countered, hoping to boost her energy back to its normal level. "I have some great news!" I added, shifting my backpack off of my shoulders and onto the floor.

I rifled through the papers until I came to the large manila envelope I was hunting down. I couldn't open it quickly enough, but finally managed to produce a collection of papers bound together neatly with a clip.

"Dad signed them!" I nearly sang.

"Ah, Nadia, your legal papers," she said. "May I?" she asked, reaching out her hand to the papers I realized I had brought to my chest as if protection was in order.

"Sure," I said, handing them to her. "He signed in every spot required, so there's no turning back now," I joked, apparently only in vain, because Dr. Ellie remained stone-faced.

"Are you considering turning back, Nadia?" she asked, turning the papers upside-down onto her lap.

I noticed for the first time how sad she looked, as if that mess of a woman had somehow transferred some of her sadness onto Dr. Ellie. I hadn't really considered it before, but even though Dr. Ellie is a professional, her clients' moods must affect her in some way. Did she ever greet clients after a session with me the way she was behaving right now? I assumed that she enjoyed spending an hour with me every other week. I'm interesting and crack a lot of jokes, but now that I think about it, Dr. Ellie *is* really smart and probably sees through my jokes. Sometimes even she can't help but give me the look I have become familiar with seeing on adults' faces: pity.

"No, it was a joke," I said, quickly adding, "Why was that woman so sad?"

"Are you talking about the woman who was leaving the office as you came in?" she asked.

"Yeah, the woman with the red sweater. She was a mess. Why was she so sad?" I asked again, more emphasis on "sad" this time.

"Nadia, you know I cannot discuss my other clients' situations with you," she said, with the hint of an appreciative smile.

"I will tell you that you are not alone in your grief. There are many, many others who are in the process of losing someone they love, either through death, divorce, or a gradual diminishing of affection. Loving others always carries with it the risk of suffering or loss, doesn't it?" she asked.

She continued on, unaware of the way I was squirming in my chair. It felt like this conversation had become about someone other than me. Someone else who had sat right where I was sitting, going through something different than I was experiencing. Someone who was a mess.

"The thing about suffering," said Dr. Ellie, refocusing her attention back on me, looking me right in the eye, "is that in those instances when we are in the depths of hurt and in pain, nearly ready to curl up in our fetal positions and give up, is when we are able to become most acutely aware of hope growing up from within us, ready to bud and blossom. Hope is there all along, growing up right alongside despair, sometimes nearly choked out as with dandelions among the daffodils. You must never allow yourself to feel ashamed at discovering hope rising up out of suffering, not when the two are rooted right there together in the same fertile soil. It's who you are. It's who we all are," she finished, leaving me feeling a bit dizzy and grateful for the sturdiness of this brown sofa, its earthy color mimicking the visual of the soil within me that I had never considered until now.

"The only question is, and the choice is yours, my dear: Who do you want to become as a result of this devastating experience? Is Nadia really going to be your salvation?" she added with a gentle prodding and even gentler eyes.

I shook my head. "I don't know how to be anyone but Hope, but it's just too late for that," I said.

As I spoke these words, I knew that I realized a truth, but also understood that I had dedicated all of my time and energy into fighting for a new identity. I wasn't sure I could turn back now.

As I rode my bike home, I realized that I had forgotten to collect my signed paperwork from Dr. Ellie in my haste to escape the seed she had planted deep within me. Its implications stirred at my broken heart, causing an ache to take the place of the dull thump-thump I had ignored for some time. The hurt was acute, as if it had been waiting there, at the surface, for my acknowledgement of its existence.

My papers were necessary, had become the salve for my pain, but recovery would have to wait until tomorrow.

Chapter 26

I woke up early. The dream again. Normally I would creep downstairs to enjoy a cartoon before starting my day, but I just lay in bed staring at the ceiling. Whoever lived in the rental house before us had covered the nubby ceiling with glow-in-the-dark stars. And these weren't the fake stars with five triangular points. These were shaped more realisitically. Circular bursts of light, with comets and planets interspersed.

Someone had taken the time to recreate some of the familiar constellations like the Big and Little Dipper, which Dad had taught me were actually named Ursa Major and Ursa Minor. As I squinted up onto the dim objects above my head, I also recognized Orion's belt.

It made me wonder about the people who lived in this rental house over the years. Were they associated with the university, like us? Obviously some had families, based on the evidence above my bed. Were they happy? Sad?

137

And then I wondered if anyone had ever died in this house. I hated to be so morbid, but I lay there for a minute thinking about final resting places.

This rental house wouldn't be so horrible a place to die. It did have some great little nooks and crannies for spirits to exist in the afterlife. In fact, I wondered if there was a spirit haunting this house currently. If my dad died, would he have to claim his territory, just to stay close to his family?

Or what if he died and there was no afterlife. What if dying was simply the absence of living? I couldn't stand to think that, if my dad died, he would no longer be able to see us. Somehow I could wrap my mind around the concept that we would never see him again, physically, but he was an adult. He had reached his full height. His ideal weight. He had grown and shaved his beard many times over.

But Milo had not. It hurt me to think that Dad might never see Milo grow a beard. Or my breasts, if I ever developed them. I wanted to think that Dad would be able to see us grow up, no matter what.

Weary of this train of thought, I got up, slipped on my robe, and padded across the hall to Milo's room. I knocked on the door, lightly, but got no response. I walked in and approached the lump under the navy blue comforter that gave him away.

"Milo," I whispered, shaking the lump.

"Mmmm," he said, flipping over.

"Milo," I whispered again, pulling the covers down a bit to reveal his head.

"What," he answered, his voice a frog.

"I woke up early," I said. "What do you think happens when people die?" I asked my snoozing brother.

"Really?" he asked, clearly irritated at the timing of my philosophical question.

"Just tell me what you think," I said, pulling my legs up to sit cross-legged on his bed, indicating my desire to stick around until he answered my question.

"Can I pee first?" he asked, hopping up and taking off for the bathroom.

I looked around the room. It too was lavender with a floral border. Poor Milo. No one had taken the time to paint his room a different color. He tried his best to hide the paint color by covering his walls with soccer posters, but the lavender color peeked through in-between the pictures of muscular, sweaty men in brightly colored jerseys.

"OK, what did you want to know?" he asked, returning.

"What do you think happens when people die?" I repeated. "I mean, do you think people come back as spirits so they can monitor everyone, or do you think dead is dead?"

"You want to know if I think that if Dad dies he will be able to watch us from heaven?"

"I guess, although I don't know about heaven - the pearly white gates and angels seem a little far-fetched - but, yeah, something like that," I said.

"Well, yeah, I guess I do believe that," he said.

"OK," I said. "I just wondered."

"Hey, Hope, I mean, Nadia," Milo said, stopping me before I exited his bedroom. "Do you think Dad's going to die?"

"I don't know," I said. But inside I had my suspicions. I had a feeling Milo did too.

I went back to my room and stood on a stack of pillows on my bed, so I could reach the stars. I pulled the stickers off and rearranged them so that they spelled out "I am here."

Somehow it comforted me.

That evening, as I was trying to zone out to "American Idol," Mom grabbed me by the hand and ushered me into her bedroom, sitting us both down on the bed, facing each other.

"I have a story I want to tell you," she said, "about Icarus, my favorite tree. It's not the largest sequoia, but close," she went on. "Before my time, a group of scientists named the tallest of the redwoods after Greek gods as a way to honor their immense size and strength."

Mom stood up from the chair, walked over to her dresser, and gently grabbed the redwood bowl, now being used as a receptacle for random scraps of paper, I noticed. She joined me on her bed, cutting the distance between us.

"Each of them is deeply rooted, prepared to hold steady against the worst winds and hardest rains. I've always loved this particular tree because, as legend has it, Icarus couldn't bear the idea that the glowing orb in the sky was out of his reach. He decided to create a set of wings and fly to the sun, despite the warnings of his parents and friends. Well, Icarus made it! I can imagine him up there, circling the sun, eyes closed, smirking in delight, soaking in those hot rays," Mom said, mimicking his flying movements.

"It didn't last long, this adventure of Icarus', because his wings were held on with wax, which melted when he approached the sun. Icarus must have realized too late that he was flightless so he fell to the earth, to his death."

Mom moved closer to me then, her eyes filled with tears.

"Don't you see, Hope, that even the sequoias are vulnerable. Icarus may be built for the weather, but even a tree can't withstand a bulldozer. You want the sun and the moon, but you can't attain them.

They're beyond your grasp. You can't change your name and expect a different result. You're going to fall, honey, and gravity will lead you right back to the cold, hard reality of cancer. We can't beat it, honey. We've tried. It's time to make our peace and brace ourselves for hurting," she finished, tears glistening in her eyes.

I looked down at the redwood bowl to discover the scraps of paper held my dad's handwriting. His notes to her. I was curious about their content, but knew I would never peek. I understood that they represented what remained of the precious life that Mom had loved so well. Scraps of paper from Dad held within the hollow of a lost tree.

৪০৫৪

April 6

Nadia,
I need you more than ever.
Love, Me

Chapter 27

When Dad came home from the hospital, he was accompanied by my mom and a large woman with warm brown eyes and freckled ivory skin.

"I'm Roberta," she said with a hint of sorrow, touching my arm. "I work with Hospice, and I'm here to make sure your dad is comfortable."

With that, Roberta sought out Milo, who was in the kitchen heating up lunch. I heard him ask, "How much time?" but didn't wait for the answer. I walked briskly up to my bedroom and turned on the radio just in time to hear the news of the day: armed robbery at the gas station on Sixth and Washington, abandoned baby found in the linens aisle at Sears. I quickly turned off the radio and sat down to my journal. Aside from first entry in which I noted my response to being sleepy a few months ago, it was blank. Everything was blank.

When the aroma of chicken and noodles was more than I could

bear, I ventured back down to the living room. I was surprised to see Mom and Roberta making hospital corners with sheets on an actual hospital bed, right in the middle of our living space.

"What is that doing here?" I demanded. Mom looked up, smiled wearily, and tucked a stray hair back behind her ear.

"It's for Dad," she said. "He's going to be here now." I noticed that she did not say "sleeping here" and pointed this out.

Roberta nodded to Milo, who was serving up helpings of chicken and noodles onto four plates. I did the mental math: one for me, one for Milo, one for Mom, one for Dad. Then I remembered, Mom hadn't clarified my concern about Dad's sleeping arrangements.

Was this what she was trying to tell me last night on her bed with her bowl? I wondered, frustrated that she hadn't been honest with me.

"Mom," I repeated, "I asked you a question."

Mom smiled again and said, "Honey, could we chat while we eat? I'm starving." I nodded, and began to ask where Dad was, but Roberta sat in Dad's spot at the kitchen table and I quickly recalculated the mental math I had done a moment earlier.

"Honey, Roberta is going to help us get Dad comfortable because the doctors say there is nothing more they can do to help him fight the cancer."

"But he was improving on Saturday," I said. "The doctors were amazed, remember?"

"Yes," said Mom. "They were amazed at how well he was doing at that time, and he is still alert and doing well, but it's all relative. He is doing well for a dying man."

Roberta jumped in then, "Hope, I want to explain…"

"Nadia," I interrupted. "Please call me Nadia."

"OK, Nadia," said Roberta, glancing at my mom, who scowled and shook her head slightly, in frustration, "I know this is hard to hear,

144

but I am here to help your dad remain comfortable through his final stage. I have helped several families during this process, and I want you to know that it is an honor for me to be here assisting your dad through this transition."

Transistion? Like he was a freakin' caterpillar turning into a butterfly!

"For right now, we are giving your dad liquid nourishment to keep him strong and alert. As the days pass, he will no longer ask for it and at that point we'll switch to ice. You can help feed him ice chips, if you like, but the most important thing you can do right now is to continue being Hope. Uh, I mean, Nadia," she clarified after getting the evil eye from me.

"So how long does he have?" I asked which must have surprised Mom, because she snapped her head up and looked me right in the eyes.

"It's hard to say exactly," said Roberta. "I would guess about two weeks, based on his pain levels and nutritional intake. A lot of it is up to him. He won't pass on until he's good and ready."

Quietly, Mom added, "It could be any day now."

છ૭ભ

I have to say, Roberta was not someone I expected to like. Not even a little. It was hard to hold a grudge, though, when she was so honest with me. Every question I asked her about Dad's "process," she answered as if I were just another adult in the room. She told me not to be concerned, for example when I noticed Dad trying to kick off the covers.

"I've seen folks in the final stage who couldn't stand the feel of anything on them. Even underwear."

All right, so this was a little too much information, as far as I was concerned, but I did pull the covers down for Dad and unbuttoned the top button on his pajamas just the same. He smiled at me, a smile I didn't recognize, lost in the abundant folds of skin on his once-handsome face. I smiled back.

"Hope," he croaked, his voice sounding parched. Could you get me some water, honey?" he asked.

"Sure," I whispered, letting the name slide, deciding that he deserved this pass.

When I returned I handed him the cup and realized that he barely had the strength to hold onto it. "Just a minute," I said, returning to the kitchen to find a straw.

I returned and located the lever on his hospital bed to raise it so he could drink his water sitting up. He smiled at me again, or grimaced. They both looked about the same.

He sipped the water eagerly, looking at me the whole time. "Thanks, honey," he said finally. "Could you just sit with me for a while?"

"Sure," I said, retreating to the kitchen to grab a chair, which I pulled up next to him.

"Can you put the bed back down?" he asked. I complied.

I sat down and grabbed his hand and we just looked at each other until his eyelids grew heavy under the sedation of morphine.

I started humming the theme song to "The Brady Bunch", a show I had recently discovered and learned that Mom and Dad both had enjoyed when they were kids. My dad opened his eyes and managed a half smile before closing them again.

I continued humming, lulling myself into a delirium as I watched my dad take hold of a deeper sleep.

I wonder if this is what parents do with their babies? I thought to myself, realizing how peaceful it was to sing another person to sleep, how soothed I felt myself.

I ran my finger along the lines of my dad's face. First his bushy eyebrows, then down along the ridge of his ever-so-slightly crooked nose. I followed the line of his lips, and watched him twitch a little as my fingers touched the top tip. I felt the breath coming out of his nose, steady and warm, as if nothing was wrong. He's just napping, I thought, wishing I could make it be true.

I looked down at my other hand, still grasping his. My fingers seemed plump next to his, so bony they had become. His fingernails were longer than he liked to keep them manicured. I laid my head down on the bed, next to his body and inhaled the new scents that surrounded him. Menthol, which helped his contracting muscles, and an earthy aroma from having gone several days without a proper bath, though Roberta gave him a sponge bath "in all the important areas" each day.

I closed my own eyes and somehow managed to fall asleep in that sitting-up position next to my dad's hospital bed.

I dreamed about a grey bird who tried to get my attention as it flew in tiny increments toward the woods. I tried to ignore it, but a brilliant blue flash of color under its wings lured me closer. I followed the bird until I realized I was right in the middle of my old dream, the dream in the woods, when I woke up with a start.

My neck was stiff. My dad still sleeping (I checked under his nose). I quietly slipped away. Like the bird with the beautiful colors hidden underneath, I had places to be.

Chapter 28

April 24th, it turns out, was the end of the process. We were all home, milling around, trying to keep busy as we had for the past three weeks. Roberta came every day and I never challenged her earlier prediction. I don't know if I believed that Dad would pull through, because this skeletal version of the man who used to be my dad did not even have the strength to open his eyes. But I did stay focused on each day beyond that two-week timeframe Roberta had given me. She said two weeks. It had been three. If she could be wrong about the time frame, surely there was a chance the doctors could be wrong…

Every day of the Hospice arrangement, with Dad in the living room, in the hospital bed, I would pull up a kitchen chair and sit with him and read. Just whatever was close by. One day I read a *Better Homes and Gardens* article about the care of lilacs. I tried to read *To Kill a Mockingbird*, though the subject matter felt a bit too heavy, like a rain-soaked sweater pressing against me. I moved on to my journal, sharing with Dad the private conversations I had been allowing to share with myself recently about life, love, and the absurdity of hand-knitted dog sweaters.

Dad was the only one I told about my secret crush on Malik, the boy with the beautiful smile in so many of my classes, the only other person who didn't groan when Ms. Singleton announced the poetry unit in English. Dad was also the only living person who knew I was scared to go to court. Scared to make it official. *Scared.*

We were out on the deck, Mom, Milo, and I, enjoying lemonade from the frosty mugs I had stuck in the freezer earlier, on this freakishly warm eighty degree day, when Roberta joined us.

"He's gone," she mouthed, not quite out loud.

Mom's head dropped and she heaved a big sigh, followed by a loud, muffled sob. Milo got up and went to her, putting his arm around her. I went to Dad.

He looked the same as twenty minutes ago, when I got up after reading aloud from Thoreau's *Walden*, Dad's Christmas gift to me. He had highlighted several sections of the book, and I won't ever forget the last selection we read together:

The morning, which is the most memorable season of the day, is the awakening hour. Then there is least somnolence in us; and for an hour, at least, some part of us awakes which slumbers all the rest of the day and night. Little is to be expected of that day, if it can be called a day, to which we are not awakened by our Genius, but by the mechanical nudgings of some servitor, are not awakened by our own newly acquired force and aspirations from within, accompanied by the undulations of celestial music, instead of factory bells, and a fragrance filling the air -- to a higher life than we fell asleep from; and thus the darkness bear its fruit, and prove itself to be good, no less than the light.

With these words, I had helped him be good and ready for the celestial music. I unknowingly told him it was okay to prove the darkness to be good.

He hadn't responded to any of us for the past two days, but I was convinced, now, that he had been listening. Thoreau's words had provided motivation and now everything was different.

"He's gone," I whispered, as I touched his hand, which was still warm and soft, not cold as I expected. His skin, once freckled and vibrant, was now tinged with the slightest grey. Mom and Milo joined me now, warm, soft touches upon me. We huddled up like penguins against the storm, and cried.

Together.

Hope is the dream of a waking man.
-Aristotle

PART IV - *Summer*

Chapter 29

People keep telling me to allow myself time to grieve. Well, everyone except my mom, who seems to have bypassed the stages, taking comfort in her usual routine: Get up. Take shower. Get dressed. Drink coffee. Leave heartache behind at 207 W. Spruce.

"Mom, you know that it's fine for us to see you cry, right?" I offered, tissue in hand. Even as I said these words, I wondered if they were true. Mom was our parent now. We needed her to be strong, to pay the bills, to cook our dinner. If she did break down, I wondered if it would break her.

"I don't have time to cry," she said more curtly than I expected. "Someone has to pay for you to have clothes and food. Not to mention the fact that Milo will be filling out college applications next fall. I just don't have time for crying, Hope," she said.

"Nadia," I reminded her.

"Right," she said, "and then there's that."

"What's that supposed to mean?" I asked, suddenly frustrated with myself for trying to reason with her.

"Well, you seem to be living in denial of the fact that your dad is not coming back. I'm not made of money, Hope, especially now, and to throw away perfectly good money on therapy…"

She stopped, and I watched as her face distorted to match the ugly words she had spoken.

"Oh, honey," she said, reaching for me. "I don't know what I'm saying. Don't even listen to me right now, I'm just so tired," she said as she slumped down onto one of the kitchen chairs.

"You might consider going to talk to Dr. Ellie," I whispered, afraid that I might set her off again.

She looked up at me, the same sad look I had seen many times over the past few months. "There's nothing she can say that will help," she told me. The first truly honest sentiment I can remember my mom sharing about her grief.

"Then let me help," I said, reaching out and taking her hand in mine, running my fingers over the wedding band on her left hand, turning it around and around like I used to when I was a child.

"He was so proud of you, you know?" she said, smiling at me.

"He was proud of you too, Mom," I said as I felt a drop of moisture on my hand. I looked at it in surprise as I saw another teardrop fall next to the first.

Mom was crying, and everything was okay.

ഇരു

I ran into Grace Powers in the hall today at school. Literally. I was walking to class, looking down at my feet, and *BAM*, I walked right into her.

"Sorry," I mumbled automatically, continuing on my way, when I felt someone grabbing my arm. I looked up into the eyes of my "good friend" Grace, with the perfect life.

"Hey," she said.

"Hey," I said back.

"Listen," she said. "I never did apologize for acting like a brat at my sleepover and I just wanted to, well, I wanted to say I'm sorry. Not just for making you feel bad, but for everything, you know, about your dad and everything."

I kind of enjoyed listening to her fumble through an apology, so I let her continue.

"I mean, he was so young and he didn't deserve to get cancer, and, you know, die. I'm really, really sorry. I just wanted to let you know."

"Thanks," I said. And I really meant it. I *had* been weird at her house. Never in a million years would I have expected her to apologize.

"Oh, by the way," I said, "it was me who took your Chia Dog. I named him Sprout, you know, for obvious reasons. Anyway, you should know that you did a good job seeding him; the little green plants grew out just like in the commercial. He was a perfect little pet, for a week, until he turned brown."

"I thought it might have been you," she said. "I'm glad Sprout grew out. He was my third Chia Pet. None of the others ever grew."

"Yeah?" I said. "Well, he sure was cute, but, in the end, he died just the same."

"I guess that happens, huh?" she asked.

I nodded, trying to hide my trembling upper lip.

☙❧

I walked to Dr. Ellie's after school. Given that it took me forty-five minutes to get there, I'm guessing it was at least five miles,

157

but, as I've mentioned before, math really isn't my strong suit. All I know is that it felt good to walk on this, the last day of school. I was free for the summer and endless options awaited me. Of course I had no idea how I planned to spend my time, but I had two and a half months to figure that out.

As I walked down the jagged sidewalk, I noticed several big oak trees with giant root systems had displaced it in multiple spots. The power behind these living and growing plants was enough to push concrete out of its path. I thought about it as I walked, being careful not to trip on the jutted squares.

As a kid I thought of the world in one of two ways: dependable or undependable. You could depend on certain things: brothers to pester you, dinner to be served at six sharp, brussels sprouts to taste bitter, concrete to hold its shape, and moms and dads to always be there for you. The older I got, the more items from my list were moving to the "undependable" column, previously saved for things like visits to the doctor's office resulting in a shot.

When I finally arrived at Dr. Ellie's office, I noticed her wearing a red silk shirt.

"Hi Dr. Ellie," I beamed. "You look really nice in that shirt."

"Why thank you, Nadia. How very kind of you to say," she answered with a smile, guiding me into her cozy office space, where I took a seat in the middle of the couch, a spot I had never considered sitting in before.

If you think about it, the middle cushion of a couch is the loneliest cushion. Most people sit on either end of a sofa, leaving the middle neglected. It's not too often that three people sit together at once, although every Sunday night, movie night at my house in California, you would find all four of us snuggled underneath a blanket with a big bowl of popcorn and plate of apple slices, skins removed.

"Nadia," Dr. Ellie said in a sing-song voice, which snapped me back to the present reality of me in my therapist's office sitting in the middle of a couch alone.

"Sorry," I said. "I was thinking about our couch back in California. It was red, just like your shirt, with a big stain on the far-left cushion from the time I spilled grape juice."

Dr. Ellie smiled, like she could completely understand how something like a grape juice spill might happen. "Is this a fond memory?" she asked.

"Yeah," I said, pausing, "it is. We spent a lot of time on the couch as a family," I offered. "All four of us."

"It sounds like you are remembering some important times with your father," Dr. Ellie said.

I cried a little then, though I really didn't want to. I wanted to keep remembering the red, slipcovered sofa with its purply-brownish stain; the blue, fuzzy blanket that held in the warmth of our bodies; and the purple, plastic bowl that held so many servings of butter-flavor popcorn over the years that the bottom had a permanent yellow tinge.

"He was the greatest man I ever knew," I finally managed to say in a whisper.

"I know he was," said Dr. Ellie. "And he has the honor and privilege of holding that honor for as long as you bestow it upon him."

"World's Best Dad," I said, imagining placing one of those cheesy dimestore medals with the red, white, and blue striped ribbon around my dad's neck.

"Hope's Best Dad," said Dr. Ellie.

I nodded, waving my white tissue in agreement.

Chapter 30

As I've explained before, I'm no athlete. Which is why I surprised myself by waking up two weeks after school let out with the desire to run. I had never run before, not unless I was forced to, but I felt drawn to it somehow. I wanted to run and keep on running, to be graceful like those antelopes you see on the Discovery Channel (right up until they are attacked by a cheetah, that is).

I wanted to be graceful like the antelope and strong like the cheetah. I wanted to be a runner.

There were two problems with this sudden desire: I had no running shoes and no idea what to do.

I mean, I understood that it was basically a one-foot-in-front-of-the-other activity. I've seen the commercials where some athletic woman in her hot pink running shoes is running up mountains, but I didn't know if I should stretch a certain way beforehand, or how to move my arms. I just knew that I wanted to run.

So, I went to my mom's closet and dug through her shoes. She had a pair of tennis shoes, but they didn't look anything like Milo's running shoes, so I wasn't sure if they qualified. Nonetheless, they were sure to be more supportive than the flip-flops I had been wearing since school let out.

I grabbed a pair of socks from Mom's drawer and slipped on the tennis shoes. They were a little bit big, so I stuffed some toilet paper in the toes. Then I went to my room to find a comfy t-shirt. My pajama shorts would work just fine.

I threw my hair up in a ponytail, grabbed my iPod and headphones, and opened the door. It was hot and humid.

I glanced at the clock: 9:07. *It's only going to get hotter*, I thought to myself as I closed the door behind me, shutting myself off from the manufactured supply of cool air I enjoyed so thoroughly.

I scrolled through my playlists and found the one I had made for Dad when he was sick from chemo. I could still hear his voice as he told me that The Stones were his ticket back to health. I had burned a couple of his CD's onto my iPod to share with him. Hard to believe that was only four months ago.

I stopped on the front stoop to stretch, which I decided would consist of ten squats and a couple of swings of my arms. My heart was already beating faster. I was ready.

So I ran. I ran down the sidewalk, realizing that the uneven surface was competing with my attention, so I moved out onto the street. Soon I was running down the middle of the street singing "Start Me Up" along with my iPod, but likely out of tune. I ran toward the school, to see if I could make it. Before I knew it, I was there, along with the soccer team scrimmaging out on the field. I waved at Milo, and though I think he looked my way, I'm sure he didn't recognize me in this athletic form.

I kept running. I ran downtown, toward Dr. Ellie's office, which I also passed in no time. Mick Jagger was setting my pace, and we were only halfway through *Flashpoint*. I kept going, out toward the fairgrounds, where I saw trailers unloading horses, sheep, and pigs in preparation for the county fair next weekend. The animals seemed to sense my presence, for as I approached they sounded a chorus of whinnies and grunts. I'm sure they were all jealous of my freedom out here on the open road.

I passed the fairgrounds, turned a corner and headed out into the country, where the scenery immediately changed: fields of newly sprouted corn surrounded me, and two-story white, rectangular farmhouses came into view, set back from the road. I passed a bright blue barn, wishing I had my camera with me to capture a little bit of quirky in the everyday ordinary. A woman on a tractor waved in my direction, and I waved back, running with ease toward the next road sign, noticing the consistency of the numbering out here in the country: 200W, 250W, 300W.

At 350W a huge dog with the stature of a Great Dane, crossed with the feathery golden fur of a Golden Retriever, came bounding out at me from between rows of tiny pine trees. The furry beast scared me half to death, but I knew I couldn't outrun him. I stopped in my tracks and waited as he sniffed me up and down, then laughed as he tickled both my arms with his big, pink tongue, my salty sweat a doggy treat.

The dog was friendly, thank goodness, and the least of my concerns. I was thirsty. Desperately thirsty. Thirsty in a way I had never been before. I had brought no water.

I aslo realized that my feet were killing me. I sat down on the side of the road while the Great Retriever paced around me with dog-like confusion. I gingerly pulled off my mom's tennis shoes and peeled off my socks to reveal giant blisters covering each of my tender toes and

163

the backs of my heels. The toilet paper I had stuffed in the toes was soaking wet, as were my socks, which I wrung out, considering the possibility of catching a few precious drops in my mouth.

"Lo-la," a woman called. "Lo-la!"

The dog, a girl, apparently, let out a bark, but stayed with me out on the road. *Loyal, after only five minutes. Figures.*

A couple of minutes later a woman pulled up in a truck. She was young, or at least younger than my mom, with a little girl strapped into a car seat beside her.

"There you are, you crazy dog!" the woman shouted. "I thought for sure I would have to chase you down again," the woman said to Lola, noticing me for the first time, sitting on the side of the road in the gravel.

"Well hi there," the woman said to me. "Is everything OK?"

"Hi," I croaked, realizing that my parched throat made talking difficult.

"Are you OK?" she asked again, with the same look my mom had when I hit my head on the coffee table after I fell off the couch trying to swat at a fly a couple of years ago.

"I'm so thirsty," was all I could manage.

"Do you want to come back to the house with me?" the woman asked.

"Sure," I whispered, more concerned about my need for water than any horrors that might occur in a stranger's home.

"Hop in," she said, reaching across the little girl and opening the passenger door. "Handle doesn't work on the outside," she said.

I climbed in just as Lola jumped into the bed of the truck, our synchronized movements another testament to her loyalty to me.

"I'm Divine and this is my daughter, Hannah," she said as they both eyed me curiously.

I drank them in as well, so grateful for the offer of water.

When their house came into view, the first thing I noticed were the huge hanging baskets of pink flowers, which hung down like a floral waterfall. The second thing I noticed was matching hot pink door that greeted me cheerily.

I chugged three glasses of water as Divine fetched a big stew pot to soak my ruined feet in.

"Your name is interesting," I said to Divine, in between gulps.

"My parents were hippies," Divine told me, "or at least hippy wannabes. I was born in 1983, so my parents missed the sixties revolution, but I still got the sixties name," she told me, laughing. "I got lucky with Divine – my sister's name was Lollapalooza, after the music festival. Lola, for short."

"Was?" I asked, my curiosity piqued with the past tense use of the word.

"Yeah, Lola died. She was a real sweet girl, but she got mixed up with drugs and some other bad stuff. Unfortunately, she didn't even make it to graduation. She lived hard and died young," Divine told me, sparing few details. "But I loved her all the same. I named this sweet girl after her," she said, rubbing Lola the dog behind the ears.

"My dad died," I blurted out, much to my own surprise.

"When?" she asked.

"April," I said. "His favorite month. He died of lung cancer right in my living room." I said.

"Wow, that sucks," Divine said.

"Yeah," I agreed.

"I thought I'd never get over missing my sister," she said, "and come to think of it, I never have, but it does get easier. At first it just seems like your heart is being torn up from the inside out, those first few weeks. And then there's a stabbing kind of pain every once in a

165

while. After a year or so, the feelings are just different. Kind of nice, even. It stops hurting so much to remember and sometimes it even makes your heart feel good."

My heart pulsed to a steady, stabbing beat as she spoke.

"Sorry, I don't know anything about you or your dad. I should shut up and let you soak in peace," Divine said.

"No, please don't," I said, grabbing her arm as she turned to go. "I like hearing it. It's just that," I started, "well, it's just that sometimes I wish I had never even known him because then it wouldn't hurt so bad."

We looked at each other for a second or two, and I recognized the look of pity I was so accustomed to these days. But this time I didn't mind. I was sad and lonely, my heart was being torn up from the inside out. I was deserving of some pity.

So I accepted it, along with the peanut butter sandwich Divine offered up as we chatted and laughed, watching Hannah try to eat applesauce with her fingers in the high chair between us.

Chapter 31

I couldn't feel my feet for three days. The blisters got all white and puffy, and I had to wear my furry winter slippers day and night to keep from popping all seventeen of them.

My legs were worse. It hurt to walk, stand, and even lay down.

"Serves you right," my mom barked at me as I continued to complain nearly a week after my outing. "You could have been killed out there and I wouldn't have even known!"

Mom *did* almost kill me when Divine dropped me off the afternoon of my run. Of course you wouldn't know it, given how polite she was to Divine.

"Thank you so much!" she said to Divine, grabbing her hand through the truck window. "I was absolutely worried sick," she said, her other arm around my waist in a show of affection.

"I was happy to help," Divine said. "I have a daughter myself," she said, reaching over and rubbing Hannah's blonde head. "I'd like to think that the world is full of kind, helpful souls. In fact, Nadia, let me write my number down for you, in case you ever want to talk," she said, winking at me.

"What a wonderul offer," said Mom, still completely reasonable. "Nadia could use a friend to talk to," she said, looking at me through squinted eyes. *Oh boy.*

Divine slipped me a pink post-it, which I happily took from her.

"Thank you. For everything," I said, looking her straight in the eyes. "Bye, Hannah!" I waved to the child.

"Call me anytime," Divine told me. "I don't get many visitors out in the country and I'm so grateful Lola discovered you out there on the road. We were meant to meet, kiddo," she said, before sliding the truck in reverse.

We stood there waving as the truck backed up and left us standing there together.

"I cancelled my afternoon class looking for you! Where the hell were you and why the hell were you out on a country road?" my mom screamed as she escorted me by the elbow into the house once Divine was out of earshot.

"I went for a run," I said, "and got a little lost. Divine brought me home. She's nice, Mom. She understands me and she let me soak my feet in her pot." None of it made any sense coming out of my mouth, but I was still stunned at the ferocity of my mother.

"I just really can't even look at you right now," my mom said as she turned and walked back out of the house, slamming the screen door once more.

"What did you do?" Milo asked, apparently catching the tail end of the conversation.

"I went for a run," I grumbled, irritated at Mom's rudeness.

"Where?" he asked.

"I don't know, around," I said. "Out past that blue barn."

"You mean the one out past the fairgrounds?" he asked.

"Yeah, I guess," I said.

"No way," he said, shaking his head in disbelief.

"Yes way," I said back.

"The blue barn is on coach's training route. It's at least eight miles out!" he challenged.

"Yeah, so?" I shrugged, though I was in as much disbelief as Milo. I had never run a quarter of a mile, much less eight. No wonder I felt like Divine had run me over in her truck, rather than delivering me back here in its cab.

སོ་ཕྱ

While my little jaunt had created quite a bit of drama and caused me a week's worth of pain, it had still been worth it. I had sprouted wings.

I thought of Divine and opened up the drawer of my bedside table, where I had stashed her phone number. I considered calling her, but decided against it. *Maybe after breakfast*, I thought to myself.

I shuffled down the stairs into the kitchen and opened up the refrigerator, looking for something, anything, to satisfy my hunger. I settled on leftover pizza from last night's dinner. *Still no groceries*, I thought with irritation, as I remembered that Mom had yet to go to the store this week.

"Serves her right if we all get rickets," I said out loud to no one.

"What?" yelled Milo from the living room, where he was busy intercepting a pass thrown by Peyton Manning on the Wii.

"Nothing," I grumbled.

I headed back upstairs with my remaining slice of pizza and glass of orange juice (100% pulp – yuck!), venturing over to my bedside table.

I picked up the pink post-it and headed back downstairs to use the phone, then punching in the numbers Divine had written for me.

"Hello?" she said with a gravely voice which meant I had either awakened her or she had yet to talk today.

"Hi," I said.

"Hello?" she asked again. "Who is this?"

"It's me, Nadia," I said.

"Well, hi, Nadia!" she said, the gravel working its way out of her voice. "How are you kiddo? You're not making your one phone call just now are you?"

I was confused for a moment, then realized the last time she had seen me I was climbing out of her truck into a sticky situation.

"No, I just wanted to say 'hi' and thank you for the ride," I said.

"Did you get in much trouble?" she asked.

"Nah," I said. "Well, yeah, actually my mom was pretty freaked out."

"I can imagine," she said. "You really screwed up, huh?"

"Yeah, I guess so," I said. "Can I come over?" I asked before even realizing that I was inviting myself to her home.

"Well, I would love to have you out, Nadia, but you have to clear it with your mom first this time, okay? If she's cool with it, I could pick you up next Friday at eleven and you could help me make lunch. How does that sound?"

"That sounds great," I said, surprised that this grown woman was interested in spending time with a thirteen year-old. "I'll call her right now," I said, excited to see Divine again. Glad to be important enough to someone to help them make lunch. It felt amazing.

Chapter 32

I really wanted to go on another run. And another after that. Sensible runs. Short and sweet.

"Mom," I said, coming up behind her as she finished getting ready before work. She was trying to clasp her favorite necklace, a silver lotus flower, around her neck.

"Can I help?" I asked, stepping up to her.

"Sure," she said, reaching up to pull the hair up off her neck. I clasped the necklace and petted her silky hair as it fell down over her shoulders. "Thanks, honey," she said, turning to face me with a smile.

"You look nice, Mom," I said.

She turned around, her eyebrows furrowed in concern. "What do you want?" she asked.

"What do you mean," I huffed, offended. "I just wanted you to know how nice you look today. Sue me," I said, in habit, though I immediately regretted not being more careful with my words.

Her face fell.

"Okay, you're right Mom, I actually do want something," I admitted.

The eyebrows returned.

"I want a pair of running shoes," I said. "My own."

"Oh," said Mom. "Running shoes, really? I figured you wanted to change your last name," she joked, and we both laughed.

"Nope. Just the shoes," I said. "This time."

"Sure, honey, I can take you tonight after work, if you'll do me a favor," she said.

I knew it. There was a catch.

"You have to promise me that you won't run alone again. At least not ouside the neighborhood. What you did was so dangerous, I just can't... Well, I just can't stand to think what might have happened."

"But nothing happened, Mom," I argued.

"Nadia, this is non-negotiable. Promise me," she said.

"Fine. I'll run in the neighborhood," I agreed, deflated.

"Or with a friend, if you want to explore," she said.

It was my turn to raise my eyebrows.

"A friend?" I asked.

"Well, you can't stop talking about your friend with the strange name. Maybe she would like to run with you. I remember how good it felt to get out and about when you and Milo were babies."

"You mean, you're all right with me hanging out with Divine?" I asked.

"Well of course," she said. "Anyone who saves my daughter's life is OK in my book," she said with a wink. "Ok, I have a confession of my own. Divine stopped by the day after she brought you home to make sure you were all right and we had a lovely chat. You were still in bed, so I didn't wake you," she said, making me curious about what they discussed, but thrilled that Divine had followed-up.

"Mom, could we have her over sometime?" I asked. "I really want you to get to know Divine. And her daughter. I guess we would need to invite her too."

"Sure," she said, surprised. "I would love to get to know your friend better. And, yes, most of the time mothers like to include their daughters."

I wasn't sure if she was trying to imply something, but I left it alone. It was the first time we had talked without arguing since before we moved here.

I didn't even realize it, but I missed my mom.

Chapter 33

Milo dropped me off at Dr. Ellie's. He was on his way to his girlfriend's house to help her pick out paint colors. She was redecorating her bedroom. I giggled at the thought of Milo's girlfriend picking out the same lavender Milo had in his bedroom. I wondered if she knew. Probably. Milo was just the kind of person to joke about his purple room without worrying about looking like an idiot. I admired that about him.

It was hot, like ninety degrees. I could barely even stand the shorts and tank top I was wearing, even though I knew I would be chilly indoors. It drove me crazy that, in the summer, I had to carry a sweater with me everywhere I went to counteract the air conditioning that everyone in Ohio was crazy about. In California, we were much more sensible about our indoor temperatures.

I was right, Dr. Ellie's office was cold, but perfect for her black slacks and long-sleeve lime green tunic. She looked amazing in green, and I told her so.

"Well thank you, Nadia. That is very kind of you to say," said Dr. Ellie.

"You're welcome," I said, wrapping my arms around myself, chilled while waiting for my sweat-soaked shirt to dry.

"Are you cold, Nadia? There's a sweater hanging on the back of the door, if you'd like," she said, motioning behind us. "I keep it here for just such occasions."

"Thanks," I said, getting up to grab it. Perfect.

"I thought of you the other day," Dr. Ellie said, surprising me.

"Yeah?" I asked.

"Yes, I met a lovely young woman at a reception I attended whose own name was Hope. She was showing some of her pieces in an art show," she said, pointing to a small painting on her wall, bright and faded colors interspersed across a white background, with scratches of black as if sections had been scraped away. The picture made me think of a carnival, an explosion of color and movement.

"Cool," I said, meaning the painting.

"Yes, she was cool," said Dr. Ellie, meaning the woman named Hope. "In fact, I told her how much she reminded me of another young woman I knew. A beautiful and smart young woman whose life was veering in unexpected directions."

"You mean me?" I asked, a little stunned to be the focus of Dr. Ellie's thoughts outside of her work life.

"Yes, Nadia, You. Hope, the artist, reminded me of you because she had experienced a tragedy of her own. She didn't go into specifics, but she said that the color and light in her paintings is first covered in a coat of black ink, which she then scrapes away to reveal the muted colors underneath. She told me it was therapeutic to know that beneath the darkness lay something beautiful."

I didn't know what to say. It sounded wonderful and I wished I could have more of seen her artwork.

"She sounds amazing," I said. "Kind of like my new friend, Divine."

"You made a friend," said Dr. Ellie, more a statement than a question. "How wonderful! Would you like to tell me about your new friend?"

"Well, she's older than me, but younger than Mom," I told her. "She has a daughter. A baby, really. She's amazing," I said, wondering if Divine thought the same of me, but understanding that she probably didn't.

"She sounds terrific," said Dr. Ellie.

"I told her," I said.

"About your father?" asked Dr. Ellie.

"Yes," I said. "I knew her for like fifteen minutes and I told her everything."

"Good," said Dr. Ellie. "That's really wonderful, Nadia! You trust this Divine. She may just be the person you needed to reveal your beautiful colors."

"I don't know about that," I said, "but she just seemed to, I don't know, she seemed to understand, in a way even Milo couldn't. Or Mom. She understood without making me feel like I needed to feel any certain way about it. That I could just feel the way I feel," I said, not very eloquently.

"Wonderful!" said Dr. Ellie. "That's a great insight for you," she said.

I smiled. "I'm glad you think so, because there's one more thing," I said.

"What's that?" asked Dr. Ellie.

"She thinks I'm Nadia. She doesn't know Hope, only Nadia. It's working, Dr. Ellie, it's really working," I said, beaming with my insight.

Dr. Ellie looked skeptical.

"Don't worry," I told her. "I'm just saving Divine the explanation. We both know that Nadia is here to stay," I said.

"Do we?" Dr. Ellie asked, challenging me.

"Yes, *we* do," I said. End of discussion.

Chapter 34

Divine pulled into our driveway at quarter to eleven, but I was ready. Had been since ten o'clock. I shouted my good-bye to Milo and ran out the front door, to the truck. She reached across her daughter and pulled on the handle to let me in.

"How's Hannah?" I asked nodding my head at the little girl sitting between us.

"Why don't you ask her," Divine said.

"Hi Hannah, how are you?" I asked.

"Peep-peep," she said, pointing out the front window.

"Hannah was just pointing out the robin on your front lawn, weren't you, Hannah?" Divine said, giving her little girl a quick kiss on the head before backing up and driving us to her place.

"Do you like chicken pot pie?" Divine asked me.

"Sure," I said, unsure if I'd ever eaten one.

"Great," she said. "I think we have all the ingredients back home.

179

My partner is going to join us for lunch and chicken pot pie serves a crowd. I don't make it often because the two of us can't manage it without a week's worth of leftovers. Hannah doesn't do much damage yet, do you punkin'?" she asked her daughter who was singing "peep-peep-peep" next to us.

Partner, I thought to myself. Divine must have inherited some of her parent's hippy ways.

Lola joined us halfway up the gravel driveway, barking her pleasure at seeing the familiar red truck. "Ignore the smell. Lola got sprayed by a skunk Tuesday night, and the tomato juice only helped so much," she said just as I caught a whiff of the pungent after effects.

Once inside, I couldn't help but stroke Lola's silky ears as Hannah sat in her high chair, occupied by the potato Divine had given her as we got busy chopping them, along with carrots, celery, and onions for the pot pie.

"I use biscuits, but some folks use pie crust. Hope you don't mind," Divine said, and for a minute I thought she was referring to my name, but then I remembered that she was the one person who knew me only as Nadia. *A special secret between two new friends,* I thought.

"Biscuits sound great," I said.

We popped the pot pie in the oven just as Hannah became bored with her potato, throwing it on the floor, watching it bounce and roll over by the dog's food dish. "Lo-lo," she said.

"Is Lola your doggie?" I asked Hannah.

"Lo-lo," she said with more determination and a point of the finger.

"Yes, Lola is a good doggie," I said.

"LO-LO!" Hannah screamed.

"Hannah, honey, potatoes are not for doggies," Divine said, as she scooped the potato up off the floor and into the trash can, swooping in for her daughter next, grabbing her out of the high chair and twirling her around in a tight circle, causing a burst of giggles from her daughter.

"'GIN," Hannah shouted at her mother, who took another twirl.

"How did you understand what she was saying?" I asked, feeling like a bystander to a scene that was so unlike any I had ever seen.

"Hannah may not speak much yet but she communicates perfectly, don't you, Hannah?" she asked as she twirled the giggling girl one last time before setting her down.

I felt dizzy with jealousy.

Just then Lola started barking and I watched a matching red truck kicking up dust on the driveway, approaching the house. A young woman hopped out and walked our way, carrying a blue canvas grocery bag. As she entered the house through the side door, I wondered about the familiarity of this friend, who had obviously also been invited to join Divine, Hannah and I .

"Mmm, it smells wonderful in here," the woman said, as she set her bag on the counter. "You must be Nadia," she said, extending her hand to me. "Divine told me all about your running adventures last week. I sure wish I could just pick up and run ten miles," she said with a welcoming smile.

"Actually it was only eight," I said, "but, yeah, it turned out to be quite some adventure." I was still confused about who this person was, when I remembered that Divine mentioned something about her partner joining us for lunch. I assumed she meant her boyfriend, but she must have meant a business partner or something.

And then the woman crossed the kitchen to Divine and Hannah, picked up the little girl and gave her kiss. She then proceeded to give Divine a hug and peck on the cheek. I still didn't get it until I saw the way Divine was looking at her and then all the pieces came together to complete the puzzle. This was Divine's partner. Her life partner.

"Nadia, this is Susan, my partner," Divine said, offering a proper introduction.

"It's nice to meet you," I said. It wasn't the first time I had spent time with a gay couple, but I had put the picture together so differently in my mind that I was thrown off.

"It's great to meet you too," she said. "Now, what can I do to help? I heard you were making chicken pot pie, so I stopped and bought us some dessert: French silk pie! You like chocolate, don't you Nadia?" Susan asked.

"Oh yeah, I pretty much love it," I said, feeling more comfortable each minute. As quickly as I clicked with Divine, I realized that Susan was drawing me in just the same.

ഇരു

Both pies were terrific so I spent a few minutes copying down the recipe for the chicken pot pie to take home.

"My mom will just love this," I told Divine and Susan while they finished drying dishes together.

"It's so easy to make, isn't it?" Divine asked.

Hannah gave a big yawn in her high chair, which Divine noticed, whispering to Susan, "I'm going to go put Miss H down for her nap."

Susan walked over and picked Hannah up out of her high chair. Hannah snuggled in close and lay her head on Susan's chest. Susan closed her eyes and inhaled the top of Hannah's head. "Rest well, sweet girl," she whispered, as Divine stood behind them with her arm around Susan's waist.

I caught myself wishing that I was part of this family.

"How did you meet Divine?" I asked Susan, after Divine and

182

Hannah left for naptime.

"At school. Well, teaching school," she said. "We both taught high school."

"Here?" I asked.

"Near here," she said. "Divine was the best algebra teacher you could imagine. She had this uncanny ability to know exactly where kids were stumped, and could explain variables in a way that worked for each and every student. It was amazing, really. I taught English."

"You don't teach anymore?" I asked.

"No," she said, quietly, "we don't teach anymore."

"Talking shop?" asked Divine, reentering the kitchen.

She took a seat at the table next to Susan. "If we're going to sit around and chat, let's be productive too. Can you help me snap the beans?"

"Sure," I said.

"Me too," said Susan, getting up and grabbing a large paper bag next to the refrigerator, which, it turns out, was filled to the brim with fresh green beans.

"We quit," said Divine, matter-of-factly, her eyes flashing with a memory I didn't know.

"But Susan said you were a great teacher," I said, confused.

"I was. And so was Susan, but in the end..." Divine smiled, stopping herself mid-sentence. "If you put love out into the universe you get love back, right?" she asked Susan.

Susan nodded, smiling back.

"It's illegal to discriminate," I informed them. "My dad was a lawyer. I know these things."

"Wow, she's a clever one," Susan said to Divine.

"Told you," Divine said, grinning.

I beamed.

"We could have turned it into a whole legal drama, but we had just found out I was pregnant and I didn't want the baby to be born amidst all the negativity," Divine said.

"So you just quit?" I asked.

"Yes, we quit teaching," Susan said. "But sometimes giving up on one thing allows you to focus your energy and attention on something else. Maybe even something better than you had before."

"Susan started a nursery, from the ground up," Divine beamed. "From research and development to marketing plans. You are looking at a bonafide expert on all things green!"

"Well, I'm certainly not an expert, but Divine's right, I did build the business. Growing and nurturing my plants and trees makes me happier than anything else. Especially knowing that it supports my family," Susan said.

"My mom studies trees," I told them as I continued snapping beans into a tidy little pile on the table in front of me. "Or at least she used to. She actually quit to become a teacher, but I don't think she is very happy about it."

"I'm sorry to hear that," said Susan. "Sometimes life throws you little curve balls and if you're not prepared it can really bewilder you."

"Hey, I just thought of something," I interrupted. "Divine, you had Hannah, right?"

"Yep, and I have the stretch marks to prove it," she joked, patting her tummy.

"Well, if you had her and Susan is also her mother, who is the father?" I asked

They glanced at each other with a secret smile that I recognized passing between my parents every so often.

"We do have a really great story, but we're going to wait and share it with Hannah first, when she's older," Divine said.

"Yeah," Susan said, "Hannah definitely gets first dibs on that

184

one."

"Oh, OK," I said, thinking of some of my own stories. But, because mine wasn't nearly as sacred as theirs, I opened up and shared with my new friends eagerly and without fear of judgement.

Lola lay under the table, soaking up my words and a few of my tears.

Chapter 35

I ran around the block for the third time, bored with the surroundings, but honoring my mom's and my agreement. I noticed the houses around the neighborhood, some looking a little worn around the edges: paint peeling from cedar planks, eaves hanging crookedly off the rooflines, door hinges a bit rusty. I wondered how many of them were rentals, like ours.

Not many people were out at ten in the morning, but I did notice a boy about my age outside washing an old, black car by hand.

As I approached I realized it was Malik. *Malik?* How could that be?

"Hope?" he asked as I ran by, pretending not to see him.

"Huh?" I asked. *Smooth*, I thought to myself. *Really smooth.*

"Hi," he said, throwing his oversized sponge down into the bubbles, causing a big bunch of them to fly through the air and land on the driveway.

"Hi," I said.

"Do you know who I am?" he asked, pointing to himself as if I needed help understanding the question.

"Malik, right?" I asked, walking over. "Actually, my name is Nadia these days. Long story," I said.

He shook his head as if it made perfect sense to him. "You run, Nadia?" he asked.

"Yeah, I just started," I said. "I didn't know you lived here," I said, indicating the neighborhood.

"Born and raised," he said, grinning. Exposing that beautiful smile.

"We moved in last summer," I said.

"I know, we talked last summer. I think I was washing this same car," he said with a laugh.

"We did?" I asked, not remembering the conversation at all.

"Yep. In fact, I think we had this same exact conversation. Aside from the déjà vu part," he said, still grinning, enjoying himself immensely.

"Are you messing with me?" I asked, getting a little irritated.

"No," he laughed, "we seriously did talk. Trust me, I remember."

The implications of his words washed over me and I offered to help him finish cleaning the car.

"Great!" he said. "But my dad's kinda picky. We have to do one section at a time, rinse it twice, then wipe it down with a chamois."

"I think I can handle it," I said, prepared for the challenge ahead.

We washed, rinsed, and dried the car, panel by panel, just like his dad liked. When we were finished I sprayed Malik with the hose. He laughed and ran off, into the hosue, returning with two Cokes. "Want one?" he asked. I happily accepted.

We sat on the grass in the front yard and I showed him how to whistle using blades of grass, blowing with them wedged between our thumbs.

"It's my new favorite instrument," he joked.

"Do you play an instrument?" I asked, more and more curious about this cute boy with the amazing ability to make me feel happy.

"Guitar," he said. "But not well. I started taking lessons in sixth grade, but my fingers," he held them up in front of me, twirling them in my face, "are like sausages."

"Will you play me something?" I asked.

He laughed. "No way," he said. "I only play for my parents. They wouldn't dare laugh."

"I won't laugh," I said, suddenly serious.

"No way," he said.

"Well, then you leave me no choice." I reached down and grabbed fistfuls of grass, walking over to the shiny black car. I held my clenched fists over the hood of the car and threatened with a grin and nod of my head.

"You wouldn't," he said with a smile.

I allowed a few blades to fall. "I would."

"Fine," Malik said, laughing, "but I make no promises." He walked inside to grab his guitar and I caught my breath. Malik was funny and cute. He was friendly and kind. He was my neighbor and I hadn't even noticed. What had I been doing this past year? Oh, right. Well, maybe it was time to start anew.

Chapter 36

"Are you sure you want to go through with this, Hope?" Mom asked for the four-hundredth time that week.

"I'm sure," I said. "And you better get used to calling me Nadia, once and for all. Today's the day it becomes legally mine."

"OK then," she said taking a deep breath, as if oxygen would somehow better prepare her for this day. She definitely seemed on edge.

Mom rushed me off to the shower, then, and told me to be ready to leave in an hour. "Your court date is at eleven." As if I didn't know.

In the shower, I let the warm water wash over the chill that eminated from within. "Nadia," I said out loud.

I had insisted that everyone call me Nadia for a good three months now. Dr. Ellie remembered most of the time, as did Milo. The only forgetful one was Mom. "Nadia," I said again, this time with more force, "wash your hair."

191

As I addressed myself with my forever name, I realized that when I spoke to myself, inside my own head, it was still as Hope.

"It'll take some time, Nadia," I said to the ever-so-slightly cooling shower of water that reminded me it was time to move on.

I quickly finished rinsing my hair, toweled myself off, grabbed my trusty blue robe, and assessed the situation in my closet. Thinking back to California and Nadia-now-Hope, whose modeling career was sure to have expanded to include trips to Paris and Rome by now, I decided that my wardrobe was pathetic.

Nadia needs a new look, I said out loud, heading to my mom's closet to check out the situation there.

Sifting through Mom's clothes quickly reminded me that my mom is essentially a tree hugger from California. Plenty of cotton, not much couture. I sighed, and dug deeper.

"Perfecto!" I shouted, as I uncovered a pretty azure-colored party dress I vaguely remembered Mom wearing to a Christmas Party at Dad's firm one year.

It was a sleeveless tank dress, falling at about knee length, with a matching short-sleeved jacket. Not exactly the Milan runway, but good enough to mark this monumental occasion. I hoisted the dress up, quickly lifted my arms, and let the dress surround me. Looking at myself in Mom's full-length mirror, I decided that it was a little tent-like on me, having not yet filled in my A cup bra, but it looked nice, especially with the jacket over top.

"What on earth are you wearing?" Mom asked from behind me, her irritated voice cutting through the niceties I was bestowing upon myself.

"Uh, I found it in your closet. It fits."

"In what universe does that fit?" she snickered.

"Come on, Mom. It's not like you offered to take me shopping.

The only dress I even own is the black one I wore to your renewal of vows ceremony."

This shut her up.

"Besides," I said, "it's not like you were planning on wearing it anytime soon. The judge will be impressed with my maturity, dressing up for court. C'mon, Mom," I begged.

Mom sighed and shook her head softly, but agreed that I could wear the dress "so long as it ends up right where you found it by the end of the day."

I agreed, elated.

I walked out to the living room where Milo was doing his best to emulate George Harrison on Rock Band. He turned and whistled at me.

"Wow, Nadia, you look so... old!"

"Thanks for nothing," I shot back, carefully seating myself on the couch, crossing one leg over the other, acutely aware of the delicate yet tortuous qualities of pantyhose, which I had also borrowed from Mom.

"I was going to bake you a cake with your new name written on it," Milo said, making up for his snide remark. "Spice, right?"

"Carrot," I answered, "but close. Thanks, Milo," I said, pleasantly surprised by his outpouring of support.

"No problem. Hey, break a leg today. I mean, not because you're wearing heels, but..."

"I know what you mean," I said, cutting him off. "I don't need any luck, though. Court is just a formality. Dad signed the form, so I'm set." I assured him.

"I know," he said, "I remember. I just meant good luck in case things don't turn out exactly how you imagined."

He left me no choice. I stuck out my tongue at him, got up and went into the kitchen to grab my coat, my backpack containing the paperwork which would officially make me Nadia, and yelled for my mom. Within a matter of minutes we were out the door.

Chapter 37

The courtroom was so large it felt cavernous. The acoustics were astounding. My chair, when I scooted it back, resonated throughout the room.

But when the judge brought out a blue scrapbook, everything became strangely silent. "Your dad asked me to give this to you," he said, smiling at me, patting me on the hand as he handed it over.

Confused, I accepted it and noticed that my dad had entitled the book "My Hope" in calligraphy, the letters with all the loops and swirlies. Considering that my dad was never known for his artistry, the lettering had obviously taken a lot of time and probably several attempts.

Somehow he had found all of the notes we had written back and forth to each other over the past year. Interspersed were the pictures I had seen Mom pulling out of the albums before Dad died. I looked back at Mom, sitting in a chair directly behind me, crouched as if to catch me if I fell. She looked nervous, with a slight smile and concerned eyes. I realized then that something was up. This scrapbook held answers but I wasn't aware I had questions.

My eye was drawn to the first picture. It was of me laughing hysterically. I vaguely remember Dad taking the picture when he took Abby and I out for ice cream back in the spring, before the move. My mouth is so wide open that you can even see my throat and that piece that hangs down in the back, like a stalectite or something.

My mouth is what you notice first in the picture, but it's my eyes that I think my dad was really focused on. They look so happy, so joy-filled. I couldn't remember the last time they looked this way. I mean, I laugh from time-to-time and smile more often than I can help, but my eyes have definitely taken on a vacant quality lately.

Along with the few childhood snapshots, including the camping with Yogi photo, several pictures are recent, from Mom's attempts to capture me during our failed photography class. In one, I'm arguing, or at least it looks as though I'm arguing. My eyebrows are curled up on top, down in the middle, and the line between my nose is prominent.

Mom snapped it, probably as a means to get back at me, but Dad chose it for this scrapbook. Why? I look mean, hard, angry. My eyes are aglow. It's always the eyes. They define my face. They define my whole being, in happiness and in anger. My dad must have loved my eyes no matter their intent. He loved me.

I flip through the pages, observing myself through my dad's own eyes, staring up at myself in a variety of settings and with a range of emotions. It's the last picture, though, that brings tears to my eyes. In it, my dad and I are sitting together on the red, slipcovered sofa, pre-purply-brownish grape juice stain.

In the picture, Dad is reading *Rabbit Hill* to me. I'm about four years old and wearing my favorite Tinker Bell pajamas, the ones I refused to let my mom wash. Instead of looking at the pictures in the book, I am looking up at my dad. You can tell from my expression that he is the king of my castle, the peanut butter in my Reese's Cup, the whipped cream on my pudding. He is my hero, and I have lost him.

It was through my tears that I noticed the hot pink post-it sticking up out of the top, stuck to the back of the scrapbook, the same color as the one Divine had offered me with her phone number the day we met. Somehow I had missed it in my effort to see myself through my dad's eyes in this, his final tribute. The post-it said, simply:

> *Hopie,*
> *Thought you might want to know… Nadia? It's Russian for "Hope."*
> *I love you forever, Dad*

I looked up at Judge Mann, whose concerned eyes didn't prevent a knowing smile, mocking my discovery. I turned to find my mom also looking concerned, but obviously a party to this charade.

My body responded to this disaster by fleeing the scene. I ran out of the room, shoving the door open as I passed. I found the hall leading outside and followed it, running down the brightly colored carpet runner to the heavy steel door, which I flung open to deliver myself onto the courthouse steps. I took them two at a time, nearly tripping several times as I was blinded by tears and a cool rush of anger. I couldn't escape this stupid name. Hope. It was meant for me, but I couldn't live up to the pressure. I had failed.

Dr. Ellie was right, I was mad. I hated cancer, I hated the judge, I hated my mom and her stupid trees. I even hated my dad. He could have given me a clue that I was going to go humiliate myself in front of a judge in a courtroom, wasting my time and money. I hated myself for believing that Nadia had rescued me. Nadia was nothing more than

Hope in disguise.

I collapsed into a heap on the sidewalk, paying no attention to the adults walking past me in suits, offering concerned glances at the pathetic girl sobbing on the street. I cried and cried for a long time, until my tears were gone. I sighed, wiped my nose on the jacket of my mom's beautiful dress, Nadia's dress, and lay down flat on my back, staring up into the cloudy sky. I watched the cumulus clouds swirl around and thought I could make out the shape of Bones, my dog who still lived in California. Dogs have it so easy, I thought, as I lay there.

I sat up, becoming aware once again of my surroundings: cold, concrete. A man approached me and held out a handkerchief. Probably someone's father, I thought as I avoided eye contact, hoping he would leave as quickly as he came. He asked if I was OK, and when I nodded he walked away, whistling. I took a deep, shuddered breath and thought about Icarus in Mom's story. In his determination to reach the sun, he gave up everything. Changing my identity would not bring back my dad. I knew that. I had faced the same sun and lost. The wax seal on my documents had melted away and I had plummeted earthward landing hard on the cold sidewalk.

I thought about the universe, saw her as the face of my mom, crouching down, preparing to catch me when I fell. Dad was now a part of the greater universe, I realized. But was that knowledge enough? Was it time to let go? Did Icaraus struggle with that too, as the heat became unbearable in those final seconds? Did he ever think, *Close enough. It's time to turn back.*

Mom approached me then. Cautiously.

"Hope?" she asked quietly as she sat down next to me.

I nodded my head in response. "Hope," I said, looking into her concerned eyes, answering her question.

She hugged me tight and we both let the tears come until there were no more. She let me pull her down to the sidewalk and we snuggled up together, watching as the clouds continued their gentle swirl overhead.

I distinctly made out the face of my dad, the way he looked all those years ago, with hair and a wide toothy smile. His form filled out in puffs of white against the pale blue sky as I could make out his entire body, slightly rounded from consuming too many of his glorious meatballs. I pointed him out to Mom, who smiled at the memory. He smiled back at us and I realized that, in a moment like this, there was nothing else to do but smile back.

Love recognizes no barriers. It jumps hurdles, leaps fences, penetrates walls to arrive at it destination full of hope.
-Maya Angelou

EPILOGUE - *Fall*

October 5

Hope,   .

What a great day! Even though it was exhausting, you did such an amazing thing for people with lung cancer. Plus you helped Mom, Divine, and Susan get in shape – ha!

I'm proud of you for sticking with it. Did you notice the man standing at the finish line? The one with the green t-shirt and jeans? He looked so much like Dad that I had to do a double-take! Made me smile. Anyway, just wanted to tell you how awesome you are.

Love, Me

Maybe I should back up a little. After I decided that Hope would be my forever name, I decided to do something really crazy in honor of

Dad.

Yes, I had forgiven him for setting me up in Judge Mann's courtroom. Of course it would have been easier to simply tell me that I was spinning my wheels, but I think he was drawn to the idea this, his final case. In defending Hope he had left no wiggle room in his closing argument. His client was guilty of being innocent and he worked his magic until he set me free.

OK, a small part of me was still trying to live up to the name, but I was really excited about it this time. To me, Hope now meant that I could no longer deny my sadness and pain, but instead needed to focus on ways of making my experience meaningful for me and others. Dr. Ellie helped me work through a lot of this, and is the one who convinced me that in order to experience hope, I needed to create hope.

The first thing I did was ask Mom to help me plant a garden. An orderly garden, not flowers planted willy-nilly around the rental. There would be daffodils and tulips and, of course, purple hyacinths, ready to make their appearance in time for spring, to help bring beauty to a time of year forever linked with a sadness that would tug at us forever.

Mom and I paid a visit to Susan out at the nursery and we walked around together, checking out trees. I wanted to plant a tree, an evergreen variety, not only in memory of my dad, but in honor of my mom and her good work with the redwoods. Honestly, though, the main reason was that I wanted to get dirty, to feel the soil between my fingernails, and create life. I wanted to give Mom a seed of hope to stow away in her redwood bowl, so that its presence in our house, in our lives, chronicled her journey of loss appropriately.

After all, hope and despair come from the same place, deep within. I learned that. I also learned that dandelions were likely to sprout up among the daffodils, but I wasn't too worried. We had a trowel.

My next idea came from an entirely different place within me. With all the running in circles I managed to do last year, I thought that organizing a race would be appropriate. I had never run a race before, but I was sure hooked on running. I loved how I could push my body to do things it never thought possible. And didn't cancer work in much the same way? I decided to pair the two as a way to offset the good with the bad.

I wanted to run for cancer.

First I talked to Mom and Milo to see if they were willing to run with me, and they both agreed, though it took Mom a few days before I got an official "yes." As running seemed to be Milo's natural state of movement, he quickly jumped on board.

Next, I called Dad's partners at Bright, Carver, and Williamson back in California and asked if they would be willing to sponsor me in a run. Harv Williamson had flown in for Dad's funeral, handed me his business card, and told me to call him if I ever needed anything. I decided to take him up on the offer. He asked a lot of questions about the run, and what the firm could do to help. I told him about my idea and he, Connie Bright, and Steve Carver donated two thousand dollars in Dad's name to help me launch the first annual "Run for Your Lungs" 5K to raise funds for lung cancer research.

We recruited over forty volunteers to help the day of the race, Lucky's Bakery donated three hundred muffins, Pop's Printing donated its services for my fliers, and two hundred and forty nine individuals showed up to run for my Dad.

My favorite runner was a woman named Marilyn who had been in remission for two years. She personally thanked me for my hard work and for inspiring her to push her body in new ways (as if she hadn't been pushed enough). I was so glad to meet her, even if she did fly past me right out of the starting line!

Divine and Susan were very patient in allowing me to help them train. I created a program on my computer with a weekly spreadsheet of the distances they needed to run in order to be ready for the big day. They even bought one of those three-wheeler jogging strollers for Hannah, who, with her "Hope Wins" t-shirt, won the hearts of our many bystanders, though not the race.

Mom, Milo and I had become close friends with Divine, Susan, and Hannah. We had regular get-togethers every Wednesday night. Divine was teaching me all of her kitchen secrets, while Milo taught Hannah how to blow raspberries. It felt great to have them in our lives, especially now that they knew the real me: Hope. I dreaded telling Divine, since I had betrayed her right from the beginning.

When I did tell her she just shrugged and hugged me, telling me how proud of me she was. "I'm so confused," I told her. "I thought you would be upset and want to end our friendship."

She told me I watched too much TV. "True friends stick by each other, no matter what," she said.

And even though Dr. Ellie is officially my therapist, I also consider her a friend. She and her husband, Wally, were there, and even though it felt a little strange to see Dr. Ellie out in public with her husband, I was so glad to meet him in person. It was the first time I had seen him, aside from the snapshots I had seen in her office next to the strategically placed tissue boxes. He was handsome, with curly brown hair and the nicest dimples. He looked nothing like my dad, but reminded me of him all the same. He was speedy quick, finishing the race in 18:29. Susan's nursery, Greener Pastures, another one of my sponsors, had donated a gift certificate in the amount of two hundred dollars for the first place winner, and I was thrilled at the thought of Dr. Ellie and her husband planting one of Susan's beautiful trees in their own back yard. It was as if my dad would live on for each of us through this sense of connection: me, Mom, Milo, Divine, Susan, Hannah, Dr. Ellie, and now Wally.

At my last counseling appointment, I told Dr. Ellie that I seemed to notice parts of Dad in everyone I came across: the woman with the striped paper hat behind the deli counter at the grocery, the man holding the blue umbrella in line at the movies, the boy throwing a fit at the shoe store (he wanted blue, but they were out of his size). I think the common denominator is that each of these folks is alive, really alive. In my mind, Dad becomes alive in the random faces of my neighbors, in their expressions of kindness, curiosity, joy, and frustration.

Dr. Ellie says that I am doing great. She especially likes how I project memories of my dad onto others, says I'm a natural at picking up on the beauty in the people who surround me.

I told her that I feel like Dad is all around. And in a way he is. I believe that Dad is always with me, waiting for me to sense him. It's not creepy at all, but when the breeze was gentle on me before the race this morning, I could feel him. When I noticed the hydrangeas' purple-blue blooms in Divine's front garden, I could see him. When Grandma stopped by last weekend and made us pasta and meatballs, I could taste him. And when Malik strums his guitar for my ears only, I can hear him. It may sound a little weird, but these moments when my senses come alive, like with the color red, or the pungent aroma of basil, is when I think of him vividly. And I smile.

Mom, Milo, and I passed the finish line in 36:24, news photographers flashing their cameras in an attempt to capture the moment. Milo carried on a normal conversation the whole time, Mom could barely breathe, and I felt like I was doing something huge and really important. I grinned really big the whole time; my eyes shining bright!

Oh, yeah, I almost forgot to mention, but as I crossed the finish line I reached up and ran my fingers through my super-short hair. I cut it off on Dad's birthday last month and donated sixteen inches to Locks of Love. When I looked at the picture in the paper the next day, I saw myself grinning at the finish line, surrounded by family and friends.

As I looked more closely at the grainy black-and-white photo, I noticed a few things about myself: yes, there was some sadness, but I also noticed more courage than I could have imagined, a lifetime of possibility, and a great deal of my dad right around the eyes!

Resources:

www.americancancersociety.org

Together with millions of supporters, the American Cancer Society (ACS) saves lives and creates a world with less cancer and more birthdays by helping people stay well, helping people get well, by finding cures, and by fighting back.

www.kidskonnected.org

Providing friendship, understanding, education and support for kids and teens who have a parent with cancer or have lost a parent with cancer.

www.goodtherapy.org

Helping people find therapists and advocating for ethical and healthy therapy and marriage counseling practices.

www.appleseeds.org/100_journaling.htm

One hundred benefits of journaling.

A Word of Thanks

Hope's story lived on the fringes of my mind for several years, and a few individuals went above-and-beyond encouraging me to put it to print.

My mom and dad didn't flinch when I explained my plans to self-publish a book. With offers to host book-signings and tweets to *The Ellen Show*, your unwavering support means the world to me!

My girlfriends Amy, Laurie, and Pam listened patiently while I made excuses for procrastinating then told me to get back to work. Thank you, I needed it!

My editorial team consisted of Rachel Gentry, Connie Goeke, Lee Ann Goeke, Kerri Pickel, Ed Proudfoot, Julie Proudfoot, Tony Proudfoot, Julie Scott, and Amy Smith. You challenged me to take Hope's story to a higher level with your honest reflections and wise insights. Thanks for investing in Hope and viva la red pen!

Amy Smith gave the final thumbs-up. Your eye for detail gave me the confidence to move forward. Thank you, and may you always have your choice of seating!

Julie Scott not only designed my beautiful cover, but introduced me to CreateSpace, helping guide me through the publication process. Your experience made all the difference. Thank you for dragging me to the finish line: "Hope Wins!"

My husband and daughters tolerated my ongoing insecurities around this project with loving support and Thai take-out when I couldn't be torn away from my laptop. You three truly are the peanut butter in my Reese's Cup!

Finally, a nod to the organizers of NaNoWriMo for providing the discipline and structure I needed to complete a half-finished piece of work in a month.

Natalie

Natalie Proudfoot lives in Indiana with her husband and two daughters. With an MS in counseling, she enjoys spending time getting to know people of all ages, learning about issues that impact them, and discovering what is important in the lives they lead. This is her first novel.

You can find more of her writing at:
http://proudliving.wordpress.com
Like proudliving on Facebook
Follow proudliving on Twitter

Natalie's second youth novel is in the works:

Sixteen year-old "Dino" is larger than life. Adored by his friends, he struggles with obesity and the reasons behind his emotional eating. It is not until an accidental encounter with a stray mutt that he begins to see himself as worthy of a new, healthier lifestyle.

Made in the USA
Lexington, KY
14 June 2012